JOHN PAUL II

THE POPE'S CHALLENGE

Scepter

New York — London

Cover: Ken Regan - Camera 5

ISBN 0-933932-33-2

CONTENTS

WASHINGTON, D.C.

Introduction

HIS HOLINESS, Pope John Paul II, delivered 53 addresses (generally to specific groups) during his 2,500 mile pastoral visit in the United States from October 1 to 7, 1979 (4 in Boston, 15 in New York, 7 in Philadelphia, 2 in Des Moines, 9 in Chicago, and 16 in Washington). Approximately 15 million people heard him in person or saw him directly as he passed among us, and virtually the entire population saw or heard him via the media of communication.

The Holy Father brought to America a message of challenge: a challenge to the nations of the world; a challenge to American Catholics; a challenge to the hierarchy, priests and religious; a challenge to all Americans. Pope John Paul II spoke of the need for conversion and rededication, the need for a commitment to live according to the Gospel. His challenge, while demanding, was at the same time joyful, because it is precisely in the struggle to live according to the Gospel message that one finds the peace and joy which Christ brought to the earth. As the

Holy Father repeated on a number of occasions, "We are an Easter people, and Alleluia is our song."

These homilies and addresses were directed to American Catholics in particular and to all men in general—individuals, families, congregations, corporate societies, communities, and the nation as a whole. With a joyful countenance and a firm voice he spoke about God and God's ways, reaching above all barriers and differences. He embraced within his orbit men and women, old and young, rich and poor, Catholics and non-Catholics; the clergy and lay people, bishops, priests, seminarians, brothers, sisters; people in public and in private life, members of diverse professions (specifically teachers and students, diplomats and politicians, scholars and journalists, artists and farmers). He addressed as personally as the crowded circumstances permitted persons of every situation and condition, the diverse ethnic and racial groups (specifically Polish, Irish, Italians, Latin Americans, and Blacks), and the representatives of all the peoples of the world, those of the Western hemisphere in particular. He took his catechetical message into the highest councils of state and into the most miserable slums, into the teeming metropolis and the quiet countryside.

Though his tone and approach were always positive and kindly, never seeking provocations or making condemnations, he made it abundantly clear to Catholics and non-Catholics alike that he had come to reaffirm and to apply the authentic teaching of the Church. It was his responsibility to do so, he said once and again, as the universal pastor, the successor of Peter, and the one who takes the place of Jesus Christ on earth. Indeed, his presence in America seemed to re-enact the preaching of Jesus in Galilee and Judea (by the shore—Lake Michigan; in the fields—Iowa; in the temple—Washington). His talks were at once evangelical and documentary: He took his themes from the *Gospel* texts and referred constantly to ecclesiastical or civil *documents* which taught the same message he was presenting (especially Vatican II). His addresses also commented upon and enlarged what he had already written in his first encyclical letter and elsewhere.

In his role of universal pastor and head of the Church, the Pope gave to his discourses an overall unity as he returned over and over to the same themes. Beginning with the needs and the condition of *man,* he showed how the reality of *Jesus Christ* in the *Gospels* and union with Him in His *Church* is the one option that promises human fulfillment. He focused the Christian life around the theological virtues of *faith, hope,* and *charity,* the sacraments (especially the *Eucharist* and *confession, Holy Orders* and *Matrimony*), and *prayer.* He stressed the need to proclaim and safeguard the *truth,* and to understand and live in *freedom.* Invariably his homilies and other pastoral addresses concluded with a reference to *Mary,* the Mother of the Church and the secure path to God, to whom he entrusted his apostolic mission.

Other themes (peace, justice, unity) were prominent when he addressed political assemblies. To a secular audience in the United Nations (perhaps the most secular place of all), the Pope preached the primacy of spiritual over material values. To a clerical audience (all of the bishops of the United States), he insisted upon absolute fidelity to the deposit of Christian doctrine and the teaching Magisterium of the Church which interprets and applies it. And to his largest audience, near the center of the country (by the lake in Chicago), he proclaimed the crucial importance of unity among Christians as a basis for effective evangelization, the fulfillment of Christ's mission.

Included in this volume are all sixteen of the Pope's major addresses in this country and a large number of his short addresses to special groups. Some of his shorter remarks have been omitted because they consisted of only a few sentences of greetings and of special references to the group being addressed.

My Pilgrimage
to America

In his Wednesday audience on October 17, 1979, the day after the first anniversary of his pontificate, John Paul II, referred to his visit to Ireland and the United States as "a pilgrimage to the living shrine of the People of God." We include here the part of his remarks which dealt with his trip to the United States as an introduction to this collection of his addresses in this country.

"The bishop who visits the communities of his Church is the true pilgrim who arrives every time at that particular shrine of the Good Pastor, which is the People of God, participating in Christ's royal priesthood. This shrine, in fact, is every man, whose 'mystery' can be explained and solved only in the mystery of the Word incarnate. *Gaudium et Spes,* n. 22'' (cf. *Segno di contraddizione,* p. 160).

I was offered the opportunity to pronounce the above-mentioned words in the Matilda chapel, when Pope Paul VI invited me to preach the spiritual exercises in the Vatican.

These words come to my mind again today, since they seem to contain what was the most essential content of

1

my journey to Ireland and to the United States, a journey occasioned by the invitation of the Secretary General of the United Nations.

This journey, in both its stages, was actually a real *pilgrimage to the living shrine of the People of God.*

If the teaching of the Second Vatican Council permits us to look in this way at every visit of the Bishop to a parish, the same can be said also of that visit of the Pope. I think I have a special duty to express myself on this subject. It is also my deep wish that those who received me, with such hospitality, may know that I tried to become intimate with that mystery that Christ, the Good Shepherd, has molded and continues to mold in their souls, their history and their community...

I wish to thank them all for the welcome they gave me; for their response to this visit, this presence, necessarily a short one. I confess that I was surprised by this welcome and this response. We persisted in pouring rain during the Mass for the young, the first evening, at Boston. The rain accompanied us along the streets of that city, as also along the streets of New York, among the skyscrapers. That rain did not prevent so many men of goodwill from *persevering in prayer,* from waiting for the moment of my arrival, for my word and my blessing.

Unforgettable

Unforgettable for me are the districts of Harlem, with its Negro population in the majority; South Bronx, with the newcomers from Latin-American countries; the meeting with the young in Madison Square Garden and in

Battery Park in torrential rain and a raging storm, and in the stadium at Brooklyn, when the sun finally appeared. And the preceding day the vast Yankee Stadium, packed full for participation in the Eucharistic liturgy. And then: illustrious Philadelphia, the first capital of the independent States with *its bell of freedom,* and perhaps nearly two million participants in the afternoon Mass, in the very center of the city. And the meeting with rural America at Des Moines. Afterwards Chicago, in which it was possible, in a more appropriate way, to develop the analogy on the subject *"E pluribus unum."* Finally, the city of Washington, the capital of the United States, with all its heavy program, up to the last Mass with the Capitol in the background.

The Bishop of Rome, in the steps of the Good Shepherd, entered as a pilgrim His sanctuary in the new continent and tried to live, together with you, the reality of the Church, which emerges from the teaching of the Second Vatican Council, with all the depth and rigor this doctrine brings with it. It seems, in fact, that all that was accompanied above all by *great joy,* at the fact *that we are this Church;* that we are the People, to whom the Father offers redemption and salvation in his Son and in the Holy Spirit. Joy at the fact that—among all the tensions of modern civilization, of the economy and politics—there exists precisely this dimension of human life on the earth; and that we participate in it. Although our attention is directed also to these tensions, which we wish to solve in a human and worthy way, the divine joy of the People, which becomes aware that it is the People

3

of God, and that as such it seeks its own unity, is, however, greater and full of hope.

At the United Nations

In this context, also the words spoken before the *United Nations* became a particular fruit of my pilgrimage over these important stages of the history of the whole Church and of Christianity. What else could I say before that supreme "Forum" of a political character, but what constitutes the very core of the Gospel message? The words of a great love for man, which lives in the communities of so many peoples and nations, within the frontiers of so many states and political systems. If political activity, in the dimensions of the single states and in international dimensions, must insure a real primacy of man on earth, if it must serve his real dignity, the *witness of the spirit and of truth* borne by Christianity and the Church, is necessary. And therefore, on behalf of Christianity and the Church, I am grateful to all those who wished to listen to my words at the U.N. in New York on October 2, 1979.

In the same way I am deeply grateful for the welcome that the President of the United States, Mr. Jimmy Carter, gave me on October 6 at the historic meeting in the White House with him and his dear family, and with all the high authorities gathered there.

"We are unworthy servants; we have only done what was our duty" (Lk. 17:10). This is what Christ taught his apostles. I, too, with these words that spring from my deepest conviction, conclude my allocution today, the necessity of which was dictated by the importance of my recent journey. Let me repay, at least in this way, the great debt I have contracted to the Good Shepherd and to those who opened up the ways of my peregrination.

BOSTON

*In Boston, at the outset of his pilgrimage, the Holy Father proposed
to young people the option of love, and to all people, to follow
him in the name of Christ.*

Come, Follow Me

Homily of the Mass on Boston Common, October 1, 1979.

Earlier today, I set foot on the soil of the United States of America. In the name of Christ I begin a pastoral journey that will take me to several of your cities. At the beginning of this year, I had the occasion to greet this continent and its people from a place where Christopher Columbus landed; today I stand at this gateway to the United States, and again I greet all of America. For its people, wherever they are, have a special place in the love of the Pope.

I come to the United States of America as successor of Peter and as a pilgrim of faith. It gives me great joy to be able to make this visit. And so, my esteem and affection go out to all the people of this land. I greet all Americans without distinction; I want to meet you and tell you all— men and women of all creeds and ethnic origins, children and youth, fathers and mothers, the sick and the elderly— that God loves you, that he has given you a dignity as human beings that is beyond compare. I want to tell everyone that the Pope is your friend and a servant of your humanity. On this first day of my visit, I wish to express my esteem and love for America itself, for the experience that began two centuries ago and that carries the name "United States of America"; for the past achievements of this land and for its dedication to a more just and human future; for the generosity with which this country has offered shelter, freedom and a chance for betterment to all who have come to its shores; and for the human solidarity that impels you to collaborate with all other nations so that freedom may be safeguarded and full human advancement made possible. I greet you, America the beautiful!

I am here because I wanted to respond to the invitation which the secretary general of the United Nations organization first addressed to me. Tomorrow I shall have the honor, as guest of the United Nations, to go to this supreme international forum of nations and to deliver an address to the General Assembly: to make a plea to the whole world for justice and peace—a plea in defense of the unique dignity of every human being. I feel highly honored by the invitation of the U.N. secretary general. At the same time I am conscious of the greatness and importance of the challenge that this invitation brings with it. I have been convinced from the very first that this invitation by the United Nations should be accepted by me as bishop of Rome and pastor of the universal church of Christ.

And so, I express my deep gratitude also to the hierarchy of the church in the United States, who joined in the initiative of the United Nations. I have received many invitations from individual dioceses, and from different regions of this country, as well as from Canada. I deeply regret that I am unable to accept all the invitations; I would willingly make a pastoral visit everywhere, if it were possible. My pilgrimage to Ireland on the occasion of the centenary of the shrine of Our Lady at Knock constituted a fitting introduction to my visit with you. I sincerely hope that my whole visit in the United States will be seen in the light of the Second Vatican Council's "Constitution on the Church in the Modern World."

And tonight I am deeply pleased to be with you on Boston Common. In you I greet the city of Boston and all its people, as well as the commonwealth of Massachusetts and all its civil authorities. With special warmth, I greet here Cardinal Medeiros and the whole Archdiocese of Boston. A special remembrance links me with the city, for three years ago, at the invitation of its divinity school, I had the opportunity to speak at the University of Harvard. As I recall this memorable event, I wish to express once again my gratitude to the authorities of Harvard and to the dean of the divinity school for that exceptionally valuable opportunity.

To the young people

During my first visit in the United States as Pope, on the eve of my visit to the United Nations organization, I now wish to speak a special word to the young people that are gathered here.

Tonight in a very special way, I hold out my hands to the youth of America. In México City and Guadalajara

I met the youth of Latin America. In Warsaw and Cracow I met the youth of Poland. In Rome I meet frequently groups of young people from Italy and from all over the world. Yesterday I met the youth of Ireland in Galway. And now with great joy I meet you. For me, each of these meetings is a new discovery.

Again and again I find in young people the joy and enthusiasm of life, a searching for truth and for the deeper meaning of the existence that unfolds before them in all its attraction and potential.

Tonight, I want to repeat what I keep telling youth; you are the future of the world, and "the day of tomorrow belongs to you." I want to remind you of the encounters that Jesus himself had with the youth of his day. The Gospels preserve for us a striking account of a conversation Jesus had with a young man. We read there that the young man put to Christ one of the fundamental questions that youth everywhere ask: "What must I do...?" (Mk. 10:17), and he received a precise and penetrating answer. "Then, Jesus looked at him with love and told him... Come and follow me" (Mk. 10:21). But see what happens: The young man, who had shown such interest in the fundamental question "went away sad, for he had many possessions" (Mk. 10:22). Yes, he went away, and—as can be deduced from the context— he refused to accept the call of Christ.

The deeply penetrating event, in its concise eloquence, expresses a great lesson in a few words: It touches upon substantial problems and basic questions that have in no way lost their relevance. Everywhere young people are asking important questions—questions on the meaning of life, on the right way to live, on the true scale of values: "What must I do...? "What must I do to share in everlasting life?" This questioning bears witness to your thoughts, your consciences, your hearts and wills. This questioning tells the world that you, young people, carry within yourselves a special openness with regard to what is good and what is true. This openness is, in a sense, a "revolution" of the human spirit. And in this openness you can all experience in some measure what the young man in the Gospel experienced: "Jesus looked at him with love" (Mk. 10:21).

Heed the call of Christ

To each one of you I say, therefore: Heed the call of Christ when you hear him saying to you: "Follow me!" Walk in my path! Stand by my side! Remain in my love! There is a choice to be made: a choice for Christ and his way of life, and his commandment of love.

The message of love that Christ brought is always important, always relevant. It is not difficult to see how today's world, despite its beauty and grandeur, despite the conquests of science and technology, despite the refined and abundant material goods that it offers, is yearning for more truth, for more love, for more joy. And all of this is found in Christ and in his way of life.

Do I then make a mistake when I tell you, Catholic youth, that it is part of your task in the world and the church to reveal the true meaning of life where hatred, neglect or selfishness threaten to take over the world? Faced with problems and dissapointments, many people will try to escape from their responsibility: escape in selfishness, escape in sexual pleasure, escape in drugs, escape in violence, escape in indifference and cynical attitudes. But today, I propose to you the option of love, which is the opposite of escape. If you really accept that love from Christ, it will lead you to God. Perhaps in the priesthood or religious life; perhaps in some special service to your brothers and sisters: especially to the needy, the poor, the lonely, the abandoned, those whose rights have been trampled upon, or those whose basic needs have not been provided for. Whatever you make of your life, let it be something that reflects the love of Christ. The whole people of God will be all the richer because of the diversity of your commitments. In whatever you do, remember that Christ is calling you, in one way or another, to the service of love: the love of God and of your neighbor.

And now coming back to the story of the young man in the Gospels, we see that he heard the call—"Follow me"—but that he "went away sad, for he had many possessions."

Love is demanding

The sadness of the young man makes us reflect. We could be tempted to think that many possessions, many of the goods of this world, can bring happiness. We see instead in the case of the young man in the Gospel that his many possessions had become an obstacle to accepting the call of Jesus to follow him. He was not ready to say yes to Jesus, and no to self, to say yes to love and no to escape.

Real love is demanding. I would fail in my mission if I did not clearly tell you so. For it was Jesus—our Jesus himself—who said: "You are my friends if you do what I command you" (Jn. 15:14). Love demands effort and a personal commitment to the will of God. It means discipline and sacrifice, but it also means joy and human fulfillment.

Dear young people: Do not be afraid of honest effort and honest work; do not be afraid of the truth. With Christ's help, and through prayer, you can answer his call, resisting temptations and fads, and every form of mass manipulation. Open your hearts to the Christ of the Gospels—to his love and his truth and his joy. Do not go away sad!

And, as a last word to all of you who listen to me tonight, I would say this: The reason for my mission, for my journey, through the United States is to tell you, to tell everyone—young and old alike—to say to everyone in the name of Christ, "Come and follow me!"

Follow Christ! You who are married: Share your love and your burdens with each other; respect the human dignity of your spouse; accept joyfully the life that God gives through you; make your marriage stable and secure for your children's sake.

Follow Christ! You who are single or who are preparing for marriage. Follow Christ! You who are young or old. Follow Christ! You who are sick or aging; who are suffering or in pain. You who feel the need for healing, the need for love, the need for a friend—Follow Christ!

To all of you I extend—in the name of Christ—the call,

15

the invitation, the plea: "Come and follow me." This is why I have come to America, and why I have come to Boston tonight: to call you to Christ—to call all of you and each of you to live in his love, today and forever. Amen!

NEW YORK

Children of the United Nations International School present flowers to the Holy Father as he enters the lobby of the UN General Assembly building. At left, UN Secretary General Kurt Waldheim smiles approvingly.

Wide World Photos

The United Nations:
Forum of Truth and Justice

*Address to the UN General Assembly in New York,
    October 2.*

Mr. President,

1. I desire to express my gratitude to the General Assembly of the United Nations, which I am permitted today to participate in and to address. My thanks go in the first place to the secretary general of the United Nations organization, Dr. Kurt Waldheim. Last autumn, soon after my election to the Chair of St. Peter, he invited me to make this visit, and he renewed his invitation in the course of our meeting in Rome last May. From the first moment I felt greatly honored and deeply obliged. And today, before this distinguished assembly, I also thank you, Mr, President, who have so kindly welcomed me and invited me to speak.

2. The formal reason for my intervention today is, without any question, the special bond of cooperation that links the Apostolic See with the United Nations organization, as is shown by the presence of the Holy See's permanent observer to this organization. The existence of this bond, which is held in high esteem by the Holy See, rests on the sovereignty with which the

Apostolic See has been endowed for many centuries. The territorial extent of that sovereignty is limited to the small state of Vatican City, but the sovereignty itself is warranted by the need of the papacy to exercise its mission in full freedom and to be able to deal with any interlocutor, whether a government or an international organization, without dependence on other sovereignties. Of course the nature and aims of the spiritual mission of the Apostolic See and the church make their participation in the tasks and activities of the United Nations organization very different from that of the states, which are communities in the political and temporal sense.

3. Besides attaching great importance to its collaboration with the United Nations organization, the Apostolic See has always, since the foundation of your organization, expressed its esteem and its agreement with the historic significance of this supreme forum for the international life of humanity today. It also never ceases to support your organization's functions and initiatives, which are aimed at peaceful coexistence and collaboration between nations. There are many proofs of this. In the more than 30 years of the existence of the United Nations organization, it has received much attention in papal messages and encyclicals, in documents of the Catholic episcopate, and likewise in the Second Vatican Council. Pope John XXIII and Pope Paul VI looked with confidence on your important institution as an eloquent and promising sign of our times. He who is now addressing you has, since the first months of his pontificate, several times expressed the same confidence and conviction as his predecessors.

4. This confidence and conviction on the part of the Apostolic See are the result, as I have said, not of merely political reasons but of the religious and moral character of the mission of the Roman Catholic Church. As a universal community embracing faithful belonging to almost all countries and continents, nations, peoples, races, languages and cultures, the church is deeply interested in the existence and activity of the organization whose very name tells us that it unites and associates; it does not divide and oppose. It seeks out the ways for understanding and peaceful collaboration, and endeavors with the means at its disposal and the methods in its power to exclude war, division and mutual destruction within the great family of humanity today.

5. This is the real reason, the essential reason, for my presence among you, and I wish to thank this distinguished assembly for giving consideration to this reason, which can make my presence among you in some way useful. It is certainly a highly significant fact that among you in the representatives of the states, whose raison d'etre is the sovereignty of powers linked with territory and people, there is also today the representative of the Apostolic See and the Catholic Church. This Church is the Church of Jesus Christ, who declared before the tribunal of the Roman judge, Pilate, that he was a king, but with a kingdom not of this world (cf. Jn. 18:36-37). When he was then asked about the reason for the existence of his kingdom among men, he explained: "For this I was born, and for this I have come into the world, to bear witness to the truth" (Jn. 18:37). Here, before the

representatives of the states, I wish not only to thank you but also to offer my special congratulations, since the invitation extended to the Pope to speak in your assembly shows that the United Nations organization accepts and respects the religious and moral dimension of those human problems that the Church attends to, in view of the message of truth and love that it is her duty to bring to the world. The questions that concern your functions and receive your attention—as is indicated by the vast organic complex of institutions and activities that are part of or collaborate with the United Nations, especially in the fields of culture, health, food, labor and the peaceful uses of nuclear energy—certainly make it essential for us to meet in the name of man in his wholeness, in all the fullness and manifold riches of his spiritual and material existence, as I have stated in my encyclical *Redemptor Hominis,* the first of my pontificate.

Dignity of the person

6. Now, availing myself of the solemn occasion of my meeting with the representatives of the nations of the earth, I wish above all to send my greetings to all the men and women living on this planet. To every man and every woman, without any exception whatever. Every human being living on earth is a member of a civil society, of a nation, many of them represented here. Each one of you, distinguished ladies and gentlemen, represents a particular state, system and political structure, but what you represent above all are individual human beings; you are all representatives of men and women, of practically all the people of the world,

individual men and women, communities and peoples who are living the present phase of their own history and who are also part of the history of humanity as a whole, each of them a subject endowed with dignity as a human person, with his or her own culture, experiences and aspirations, tensions and sufferings, and legitimate expectations. This relationship is what provides the reason for all political activity, whether national or international, for in the final analysis this activity comes from man, is exercised by man and is for man. And if political activity is cut off from this fundamental relationship and finality, if it becomes in a way its own end, it loses much of its reason to exist. Even more, it can also give rise to a specific alienation; it can become extraneous to man; it can come to contradict humanity itself. In reality, what justifies the existence of any political activity is service to man, concerned and responsible attention to the essential problems and duties of his earthly existence in its social dimension and significance, on which also the good of each person depends.

7. I ask you, ladies and gentlemen, to excuse me for speaking of questions that are certainly self-evident for you. But it does not seem pointless to speak of them, since the most frequent pitfall for human activities is the possibility of losing sight, while performing them, of the clearest truths, the most elementary principles.

I would like to express the wish that, in view of its universal character, the United Nations organization will never cease to be the forum, the high tribune from which all man's problems are appraised in truth and justice. It was in the name of this inspiration, it was through this historic stimulus, that on June 26, 1945, toward the end of the terrible World War II, the charter of the United Nations was signed and on the following October 24 your organization began its life. Soon after, on December 10, 1948, came its fundamental document, the Universal Declaration of Human Rights, the rights of the human being as a concrete individual and of the human being in his universal value. This document is a milestone on the long and difficult path of the human race. The progress of humanity must be measured not only by the progress of science and technology, which shows man's uniqueness with regard to nature, but also and chiefly by the primacy given to spiritual values and by the progress of moral life. In this field is manifested the full dominion of reason, through truth, in the behavior of the individual and of society, and also the control of reason over nature; and thus human conscience quietly triumphs, as was expressed in the ancient saying, *"Genus humanum arte et ratione vivit."*

It was when technology was being directed in its one-sided progress towards goals of war, hegemony and conquest, so that man might kill man and nation destroy nation by depriving it of its liberty and the right to exist—and I still have before my mind the image of World War II in Europe, which began 40 years ago on September 1, 1939 with the invasion of Poland and ended on May 9, 1945—it was precisely then that the United Nations organization arose. And three years later the document appeared which, as I have said, must be considered a real milestone on the path of the moral progress of humanity —the Universal Declaration of Human Rights. The governments and states of the world have understood that, if they are not to attack and destroy each other, they must unite. The real way, the fundamental way to this is through each human being, through the definition and recognition of and respect for the inalienable rights of individuals and of the communities of peoples.

Torture and oppression

8. Today, 40 years after the outbreak of World War II, I wish to recall the whole of the experiences by individuals and nations that were sustained by a generation that is largely still alive. I had occasion not long ago to reflect again on some of those experiences, in one of the places that are most distressing and overflowing with contempt for man and his fundamental rights—the extermination camp of Oswiecim (Auschwitz), which I visited during my pilgrimage to Poland last June. This infamous place is unfortunately only one of the many scattered over the continent of Europe. But the memory of even the one should be a warning sign on the path of humanity today, in order that every kind of concentration camp anywhere on earth may once and for all be done away with. And everything that recalls those horrible experiences should also disappear forever from the lives of nations and states, everything that is a continuation of those experiences under different forms, namely the various kinds of torture and oppression, either physical or moral, carried out under any system, in any land; this phenomenon is all the more distressing if it occurs under the pretext of internal security or the need to preserve an apparent peace.

9. You will forgive me, ladies and gentlemen, for evoking this memory. But I would be untrue to the history of this century, I would be dishonest with regard to the great cause of man, which we all wish to serve, if I should keep silent, I who come from the country on whose living body Oswiecim was at one time constructed. But my purpose in invoking this memory is above all to show what painful experiences and sufferings by millions of people gave rise to the Universal Declaration of Human Rights, which has been placed as the basic inspiration and cornerstone of the United Nations organization. This declaration was paid for by millions of our brothers and sisters at the cost of their suffering and sacrifice, brought about by the brutalization that darkened and made insensitive the human consciences of their oppressors and of those who carried out a real genocide. This price cannot have been paid in vain! The Universal Declaration of Human Rights—with its train of many declarations and conventions on highly important aspects of human rights, in favor of children, of women, of equality between races, and especially the two international covenants on economic, social and cultural rights and on civil and political rights—must remain the basic value in the United Nations organization with which the consciences of its members must be confronted and from which they must draw continual inspiration. If the truths and principles contained in this document were to be forgotten or ignored and were thus to lose the genuine self-evidence that distinguished them at the time they were brought painfully to birth, then the noble purpose of the United Nations organization could be

faced with the threat of a new destruction. This is what would happen it the simple yet powerful eloquence of the Universal Declaration of Human Rights were decisively subjugated by what is wrongly called political interest, but often really means no more than one-sided gain and advantage to the detriment of others, or a thirst for power regardless of the needs of others—everything which by its nature is opposed to the spirit of the declaration. Political interest understood in this sense, if you will pardon me, ladies and gentlemen, dishonors the noble and difficult mission of your service for the good of your countries and of all humanity.

"War, never again"

10. Fourteen years ago my great predecessor Pope Paul VI spoke from this podium. He spoke memorable words, which I desire to repeat today: "No more war, war never again! Never one against the other," or even "one above the other," but always, on every occasion, "with each other."

Paul VI was a tireless servant of the cause of peace. I wish to follow him with all my strength and continue his service. The Catholic Church in every place on earth proclaims a message of peace, prays for peace, educates for peace. This purpose is also shared by the representatives and followers of other churches and communities and of other religions of the world, and they have pledged themselves to it. In union with efforts by all people of good will, this work is certainly bearing fruit. Nevertheless we are continually troubled by the armed conflicts that break out from time to time. How grateful we are to the Lord when a direct intervention succeeds in avoiding such a conflict, as in the case of the tension that last year threatened Argentina and Chile.

It is my fervent hope that a solution also to the Middle East crisis may draw nearer. While being prepared to recognize the value of any concrete step or attempt made to settle the conflict, I want to recall that it would have no value if it did not truly represent the first stone of a general overall peace in the area, a peace that, being necessarily based on equitable recognition of the rights of all, cannot fail to include the consideration and just settlement of the Palestinian question. Connected with this question is that of the tranquility, independence and territorial integrity of Lebanon within the formula that has made it an example of peaceful and mutually fruitful coexistence between distinct communities, a formula that I hope will, in the common interest, be maintained, with the adjustments required by the development of the situation. I also hope for a special statute that, under international guarantees—as my predecessor Paul VI indicated—would respect the particular nature of Jerusalem, a heritage sacred to the veneration of millions of believers of the three great monotheistic religions, Judaism, Christianity and Islam.

Disarmament

We are troubled also by reports of the development of weaponry exceeding in quality and size the means of war and destruction ever known before. In this field also we applaud the decisions and agreements aimed at reducing the arms race. Nevertheless, the life of humanity today is seriously endangered by the threat of destruction and by the risk arising even from accepting certain tranquilizing reports. And the resistance to actual concrete proposals of real disarmament, such as those called by this assembly in a special session last year, shows that together with the will for peace that all profess and that most desire there is also in existence—perhaps in latent or conditional form but nonetheless real— the contrary and the negation of this will. The continual preparations for war demonstrated by the production of ever more numerous, powerful and sophisticated weapons in various countries show that there is a desire to be ready for war, and being ready means being able to start it; it also means taking the risk that sometime, somewhere, somehow, someone can set in motion the terrible mechanism of general destruction.

11. It is therefore necessary to make a continuing and even more energetic effort to do away with the very possibility of provoking war, and to make such catastrophes impossible by influencing the attitudes and convictions, the very intentions and aspirations of governments and peoples. This duty, kept constantly in mind by the United Nations organization and each of its institutions, must also be a duty for every society, every regime, every government. This task is certainly served by initiatives aimed at international cooperation for the fostering of development. As Paul VI said at the end of his encyclical *Populorum Progressio:* "If the new name for peace is development, who would not wish to labor for it with all

29

his powers?'' However, this task must also be served by constant reflection and activity aimed at discovering the very roots of hatred, destructiveness and contempt—the roots of everything that produces the temptation to war, not so much in the hearts of the nations as in the inner determination of the systems that decide the history of whole societies. In this titanic labor of building up the peaceful future of our planet the United Nations organization has undoubtedly a key function and guiding role, for which it must refer to the just ideals contained in the Universal Declaration of Human Rights. For this declaration has struck a real blow against the many deep roots of war, since the spirit of war, in its basic primordial meaning, springs up and grows to maturity where the inalienable rights of man are violated.

This is a new and deeply relevant vision of the cause of peace, one that goes deeper and is more radical. It is a vision that sees the genesis, and in a sense the substance, of war in the more complex forms emanating from injustice viewed in all its various aspects; this injustice first attacks human rights and thereby destroys the organic unity of the social order and it then affects the whole system of international relations. Within the church's doctrine, the encyclical *Pacem in Terris* by John XXIII provides in synthetic form a view of this matter that is very close to the ideological foundation of the United Nations organization. This must therefore form the basis to which one must loyally and perseveringly adhere in order to establish true peace on earth.

12. By applying this criterion we must diligently examine which principal tensions in connection with the

inalienable rights of man can weaken the construction of this peace which we all desire so ardently and which is the essential goal of the efforts of the United Nations organization. It is not easy, but it must be done. Anyone who undertakes it must take up a totally objective position and be guided by sincerity, readiness to acknowledge one's prejudices and mistakes and readiness even to renounce one's own particular interests, including any of these interests. It is by sacrificing these interests for the sake of peace that we serve them best. After all, in whose political interest can it ever be to have another war?

Every analysis must necessarily start from the premise that—although each person lives in a particular concrete social and historical context—every human being is endowed with a dignity that must instead be respected and safeguarded, if peace is really to be built up.

Basic human rights

13. In a movement that one hopes will be progressive and continuous, the Universal Declaration of Human Rights and the other international and national juridical instruments are endeavoring to create general awareness of the dignity of the human being, and to define at least some of the inalienable rights of man. Permit me to enumerate some of the most important human rights that are universally recognized: the right to life, liberty and security of person; the right to food, clothing, housing, sufficient health care, rest and leisure; the right to freedom of expression, education and culture; the right to freedom of thought, conscience and religion; and the right to

manifest one's religion either individually or in community, in public or in private; the right to choose a state of life, to found a family and to enjoy all conditions necessary for family life; the right to property and work, to adequate working conditions and a just wage; the right of assembly and association; the right to freedom of movement, to internal and external migration; the right to nationality and residence; the right to political participation and the right to participate in the free choice of the political system of the people to which one belongs. All these human rights taken together are in keeping with the substance of the dignity of the human being, understood in his entirety, not as reduced to one dimension only. These rights concern the satisfaction of man's essential needs, the exercise of his freedoms and his relationships with others; but always and everywhere they concern man, they concern man's full human dimension.

14. Man lives at the same time both in the world of material values and in that of spiritual values. For the individual living and hoping man, his needs, freedoms and relationships with others never concern one sphere of values alone, but belong to both. Material and spiritual realities may be viewed separately in order to understand better that in the concrete human being they are inseparable, and to see that any threat to human rights, whether in the field of material realities or in that of spiritual realities, is equally dangerous for peace, since in every instance it concerns man in his entirety. Permit me, distinguished ladies and gentlemen, to recall a constant rule of the history of humanity, a rule that is implicitly

contained in all that I have already stated with regard to integral development and human rights. The rule is based on the relationship between spiritual values and material or economic values. In this relationship, it is the spiritual values that are pre-eminent, both on account of the nature of these values and also for reasons concerning the good of man. The pre-eminence of the values of the spirit defines the proper sense of earthly material goods and the way to use them. This pre-eminence is therefore at the basis of a just peace. It is also a contributing factor to ensuring that material development, technical development and the development of civilization are at the service of what constitutes man. This means enabling man to have full access to truth, to moral development, and to the complete possibility of enjoying the goods of culture which he has inherited, and of increasing them by his own creativity. It is easy to see that material goods do not have unlimited capacity for satisfying the needs of man: They are not in themselves easily distributed and, in the relationship between those who possess and enjoy them and those who are without them, they give rise to tension, dissension and division that will often even turn into open conflict. Spiritual goods, on the other hand, are open to unlimited enjoyment by many at the same time, without diminution of the goods themselves. Indeed, the more people share in such goods, the more they are enjoyed and drawn upon, the more then do those goods show their indestructible and immortal worth. This truth is confirmed, for example, by works of creativity—I mean by the works of thought, poetry, music, and the figurative arts, fruits of man's spirit.

Materialism

15. A critical analysis of our modern civilization shows that in the last hundred years it has contributed as never before to the development of material goods, but that it has also given rise, both in theory and still more in practice, to a series of attitudes in which sensitivity to the spiritual dimension of human existence is diminished to a greater or less extent, as a result of certain premises which reduce the meaning of human life chiefly to the many different material and economic factors—I mean to the demands of production, the market, consumption, the accumulation of riches or of the growing bureaucracy with which an attempt is made to regulate these very processes. Is this not the result of having subordinated man to one single conception and spheres of values?

16. What is the link between these reflections and the cause of peace and war? Since, as I have already stated, material goods by their very nature provoke conditionings and divisions, the struggle to obtain these goods becomes inevitable in the history of humanity. If we cultivate this one-sided subordination of man to material goods alone, we shall be incapable of overcoming this state of need. We shall be able to attenuate it and avoid it in particular cases, but we shall not succeed in eliminating it systematically and radically, unless we emphasize more and pay greater honor, before everyone's eyes, in the sight of every society, to the second dimension of the goods of man: the dimension that does not divide people but puts them into communication with each other, associates them and unites them.

I consider that the famous opening words of the Charter of the United Nations, in which the peoples of the United Nations, determined to save succeeding generations from the scourge of war, solemnly reaffirmed "faith in fundamental human rights, in the dignity and worth of the human person, in the equal rights of men and women and of nations large and small," are meant to stress this dimension.

Indeed, the fight against incipient wars cannot be carried out on a merely superficial level, by treating the symptoms. It must be done in a radical way, by attacking the causes. The reason I have called attention to the dimension constituted by spiritual realities is my concern for the cause of peace, peace which is built up by men and women uniting around what is most fully and profoundly human, around what raises them above the world about them and determines their indestructible grandeur—indestructible in spite of the death to which everyone on earth is subject. I would like to add that the Catholic Church and, I think I can say, the whole of Christianity sees in this very domain its own particular task. The Second Vatican Council helped to establish what the Christian faith has in common with the various non-Christian religions in this aspiration. The church is therefore grateful to all who show respect and good will with regard to this mission of hers and do not impede it or make it difficult. An analysis of the history of mankind, especially at its recent stage, shows how important is the duty of revealing more fully the range of the goods that are linked with the spiritual dimension of human existence. It shows how important this task is for building peace and how serious is any threat to human rights. Any violation of them, even in a peace situation, is a form of warfare against humanity.

It seems that in the modern world there are two main threats. Both concern human rights in the field of international relations and human rights within the individual states or societies.

Rich and poor

17. The first of these systematic threats against human rights is linked in an overall sense with the distribution of material goods. This distribution is frequently unjust both within individual societies and on the planet as a whole. Everyone knows that these goods are given to man not only as nature's bounty; they are enjoyed by him chiefly as the fruit of his many activities, ranging from the simplest manual and physical labor to the most complicated forms of industrial production and highly qualified and specialized research and study. Various forms of inequality in the possession of material goods, and in the enjoyment of them, can often be explained by different historical and cultural causes and circumstances. But while these circumstances can diminish the moral responsibility of people today, they do not prevent the situations of inequality from being marked by injustice and social injury.

People must become aware that economic tensions within countries and in the relationship between states and even between entire continents contain within themselves substantial elements that restrict or violate human rights. Such elements are the exploitation of labor and many other abuses that affect the dignity of the human person. It follows that the fundamental criterion for comparing social, economic and political systems is not, and cannot be, the criterion of hegemony and imperialism; it can be, and indeed it must be, the humanistic criterion, namely the measure in which each system is really capable of reducing, restraining and eliminating as far as possible the various forms of exploitation of man and of ensuring for him through work, not only the just distribution of the indispensable material goods, but also a participation, in keeping with his dignity, in the whole process of production and in the social life that grows up around that process. Let us not forget that, although man depends on the resources of the material world for his life, he cannot be their slave, but he must be their master. The words of the book of Genesis, "Fill the earth and subdue it" (Gn. 1:28), are in a sense a primary and essential directive in the field of economy and of labor policy.

18. Humanity as a whole, and the individual nations, have certainly made remarkable progress in this field during the last hundred years. But it is a field in which there is never any lack of systematic threats and violations of human rights. Disturbing factors are frequently present in the form of the frightful disparities between excessively rich individuals and groups on the one hand, and on the other hand the majority made up of the poor or indeed of the destitute, who lack food and opportunities for work and education and are in great numbers condemned to hunger and disease. And

concern is also caused at times by the radical separation of work from property, by man's indifference to the production enterprise to which he is linked only by a work obligation, without feeling that he is working for a good that will be his or for himself. It is no secret that the abyss separating the minority of the excessively rich from the multitude of the destitute is a very grave symptom in the life of any society. This must also be said with even greater insistence with regard to the abyss separating countries and regions of the earth. Surely the only way to overcome this serious disparity between areas of satiety and areas of hunger and depression is through coordinated cooperation by all countries. This requires above all else a unity inspired by an authentic perspective of peace. Everything will depend on whether these differences and contrasts in the sphere of the possession of goods will be systematically reduced through truly effective means, on whether the belts of hunger, mal-nutrition, destitution, underdevelopment, disease and illiteracy will disappear from the economic map of the earth, and on whether peaceful cooperation will avoid imposing conditions of exploitation and economic or political dependence, which would only be a form of neocolonialism.

Freedom of the human spirit

19. I would now like to draw attention to a second systematic threat to man in his inalienable rights in the modern world, a threat which constitutes no less a danger than the first to the cause of peace. I refer to the various forms of injustice in the field of the spirit.

Man can indeed be wounded in his inner relationship with truth, in his conscience, in his most personal belief, in his view of the world, in his religious faith, and in the sphere of what are known as civil liberties. Decisive for these last is equality of rights without discrimination on grounds of origin, race, sex, nationality, religion, political convictions and the like. Equality of rights means the exclusion of the various forms of privilege for some and discrimination against others, whether they are people born in the same country or people from different backgrounds of history, nationality, race and ideology. For centuries the thrust of civilization has been in one direction: that of giving the life of individual political societies a form in which there can be fully safeguarded the objective rights of the spirit, of human conscience and of human creativity, including man's relationship with God. Yet in spite of this we still see in this field recurring threats and violations, often with no possibility of appealing to a higher authority or of obtaining an effective remedy.

Besides the acceptance of legal formulas safeguarding the principle of the freedom of the human spirit, such as freedom of thought and expression, religious freedom and freedom of conscience, structures of social life often exist in which the practical exercise of these freedoms condemns man, in fact if not formally, to become a second-class or third-class citizen, to see compromised his chances of social advancement, his professional career or his access to certain posts of responsibility, and to lose even the possibility of educating his children freely. It is a question of the highest importance that in internal social life, as well as in international life, all human beings in every nation and country should be able to enjoy effectively their full rights under any political regime or system.

Only the safeguarding of this real completeness of rights for every human being without discrimination can ensure peace at its very roots.

20. With regard to religious freedom, which I, as Pope, am bound to have particularly at heart, precisely with a view to safeguarding peace, I would like to repeat here, as a contribution to respect for man's spiritual dimension, some principles contained in the Second Vatican Council's declaration *Dignitatis Humanae:* "In accordance with their dignity, all human beings, because they are persons, that is, beings endowed with reason and free will and therefore bearing personal responsibility, are both impelled by their nature and bound by a moral obligation to seek the truth, especially religious truth. They are also bound to adhere to the truth once they come to know it and to direct their whole lives in accordance with its demands" (*Dignitatis Humanae,* 2).

"The practice of religion of its very nature consists primarily of those voluntary and free internal acts by which a human being directly sets his course toward God. No merely human power can either command or prohibit acts of this kind. But man's social nature itself requires that he give external expression to his internal acts of religion, that he communicate with others in religious matters and that he profess his religion in community" (*Dignitatis Humanae,* 3).

These words touch the very substance of the question.

They also show how even the confrontation between the religious view of the world and the agnostic or even atheistic view, which is one of the signs of the times of the present age, could preserve honest and respectful human dimensions without violating the essential rights of conscience of any man or woman living on earth.

Respect for the dignity of the human person would seem to demand that, when the exact tenor of the exercise of religious freedom is being discussed or determined with a view to national laws or international conventions, the institutions that are by their nature at the service of religion should also be brought in. If this participation is omitted, there is a danger of imposing, in so intimate a field of man's life, rules or restrictions that are opposed to his true religious needs.

Year of the Child

21. The United Nations organization has proclaimed 1979 the Year of the Child. In the presence of the representatives of so many nations of the world gathered here, I wish to express the joy that we all find in children, the springtime of life, the anticipation of the future history of each of our present earthly homelands. No country on earth, no political system can think of its own future otherwise than through the image of these new generations that will receive from their parents the manifold heritage of values, duties and aspirations of the nations to which they belong and of the whole human family. Concern for the child, even before birth, from the first moment of conception and then throughout the years of

infancy and youth, is the primary and fundamental test of the relationship of one human being to another.

And so, what better wish can I express for every nation and the whole of mankind, and for all the children of the world than a better future in which respect for human rights will become a complete reality throughout the third millennium, which is drawing near.

22. But in this perspective we must ask ourselves whether there will continue to accumulate over the heads of this new generation of children the threat of common extermination for which the means are in the hands of the modern states, especially the major world powers. Are the children to receive the arms race from us as a necessary inheritance? How are we to explain this unbridled race?

The ancients said: *Si vis pacem, para bellum*. But can our age still really believe that the breathtaking spiral of armaments is at the service of world peace? In alleging the threat of a potential enemy, is it really not rather the intention to keep for oneself a means of threat, in order to get the upper hand with the aid of one's own arsenal of destruction? Here too it is the human dimension of peace that tends to vanish in favor of ever new possible forms of imperialism.

It must be our solemn wish here for our children, for the children of all the nations on earth, that this point will never be reached. And for that reason I do not cease to pray to God each day so that in his mercy he may save us from so terrible a day.

23. At the close of this address, I wish to express once more before all the high representatives of the states who

are present a word of esteem and deep love for all the peoples, all the nations of the earth, for all human communities. Each one has its own history and culture. I hope that they will live and grow in the freedom and truth of their own history. For that is the measure of the common good of each one of them. I hope that each person will live and grow strong with the moral force of the community that forms its members as citizens. I hope that the state authorities, while respecting the just rights of each citizen, will enjoy the confidence of all for the common good. I hope that all the nations, even the smallest, even those that do not yet enjoy full sovereignty, and those that have been forcibly robbed of it, will meet in full equality with the others in the United Nations organization. I hope that the United Nations will ever remain the supreme forum of peace and justice, the authentic seat of freedom of peoples and individuals in their longing for a better future.

C. Slattery

Among the 80,000 people attending Mass at Yankee Stadium in New York City, a group of the faithful receive Holy Communion from the Pope.

Not Just the Crumbs

Homily of the Mass at Yankee Stadium,
New York City, October 2

1. "Peace be with you!"

These were the first words that Jesus spoke to his apostles after his resurrection. With these words the risen Christ restored peace to their hearts, at a time when they were still in a state of shock after the first terrible experience of Good Friday. Tonight, in the name of the Lord Jesus Christ, in the power of his spirit, in the midst of a world that is anxious about its own existence, I repeat these words to you, for they are words of life: "Peace be with you!"

Jesus does not merely give us peace. He gives us his peace accompanied by his justice. He is peace and justice. He becomes our peace and our justice.

What does this mean? It means that Jesus Christ—the Son of God made man, the perfect man—perfects, restores and manifests in himself the unsurpassable dignity that God wishes to give to man from the beginning. He is the one who realizes in himself what man has the vocation to be: the one who is fully reconciled with the Father, fully one in himself, fully devoted to others. Jesus Christ is living peace and living justice.

Jesus Christ makes us sharers in what he is. Through his incarnation, the Son of God in a certain manner united himself with every human being. In our inmost being he has recreated us; in our inmost being he has reconciled us with God, reconciled us with ourselves, reconciled us with our brothers and sisters: He is our peace.

2. What unfathomable riches we bear within us, and in our Christian communities! We are bearers of the justice and peace of God! We are not primarily painstaking builders of a justice and peace that are merely human, always wearing out and always fragile. We are primarily the humble beneficiaries of the very life of God, who is justice and peace in the bond of charity. During Mass, when the priest greets us with these words: "The peace of the Lord be with you always," let us think primarily of this peace which is God's gift: Jesus Christ our peace. And when, before communion, the priest invites us to give one another a sign of peace, let us think primarily of the fact that we are invited to exchange with one another the peace of Christ who dwells within us, who invites us to share in his body and blood, for our joy and for the service of all humanity.

In the footsteps of Jesus

For God's justice and peace cry out to bear fruit in human works of justice and peace, in all the spheres of actual life. When we Christians make Jesus Christ the center of our feelings and thoughts, we do not turn away from people and their needs. On the contrary, we are caught up in the eternal movement of God's love that comes to meet us; we are caught up in the movement of the Son, who came among us, who became one of us; we are caught in the movement of the Holy Spirit, who visits the poor, calms fevered hearts, binds up wounded hearts, warms cold hearts, and gives us the fullness of his gifts. The reason why man is the primary and fundamental way for the Church is that the Church walks in the footsteps of Jesus: It is Jesus who has shown her this road. This road passes in an unchangeable way through the mystery of the incarnation and redemption; it leads from Christ to man. The Church looks at the world through the very eyes of Christ; Jesus is the principle of her solicitude for man (cf. *Redemptor Hominis,* 13-18).

3. The task is immense. And it is an enthralling one. I have just emphasized various aspects of it before the General Assembly of the United Nations, and I shall touch upon others during my apostolic journey across your country. Today, let me just dwell on the spirit and nature of the Church's contribution to the cause of justice and peace, and let me also mention certain urgent priorities which your service to humanity ought to concentrate upon today.

Social thinking and social practice inspired by the Gospel must always be marked by a special sensitivity toward those who are most in distress, those who are extremely poor, those suffering from all the physical, mental and moral ills that afflict humanity including hunger, neglect, unemployment and despair. There are many poor people of this sort around the world. There are many in your own midst. On many occasions, your nation has gained a well-deserved reputation for generosity, both public and private.

Be faithful to that tradition, in keeping with your vast possibilities and present responsibilities. The network of charitable works of each kind that the Church has succeeded in creating here is a valuable means for effectively mobilizing generous undertakings aimed at relieving the situations of distress that continually arise both at home and elsewhere in the world. Make an effort to ensure that this form of aid keeps its irreplaceable character as a fraternal and personal encounter with those who are in distress; if necessary, re-establish this very character against all the elements that work in the opposite direction. Let this sort of aid be respectful of the freedom and dignity of those being helped, and let it be a means of forming the conscience of the givers.

Seek the causes of poverty

4. But this is not enough. Within the framework of your national institutions and in cooperation with all your compatriots, you will also want to seek out the structural reasons which foster or cause the different forms of poverty in the world and in your own country, so that you can apply the proper remedies. You will not allow yourselves to be intimidated or discouraged by over-simplified explanations, which are more ideological than scientific—explanations which try to account for a complex evil by some single cause. But neither will you recoil before the reforms—even profound ones—of

attitudes and structures that may prove necessary in order to recreate over and over again the conditions needed by the disadvantaged if they are to have a fresh chance in the hard struggle of life. The poor of the United States and of the world are your brothers and sisters in Christ. You must never be content to leave them just the crumbs from the feast. You must take of your substance and not just of your abundance in order to help them. And you must treat them like guests at your family table.

5. Catholics of the United States, while developing your own legitimate institutions, you also participate in the nation's affairs within the framework of institutions and organizations springing from the nation's common history and from your common concern. This you do hand in hand with your fellow citizens of every creed and confession. Unity among you in all such endeavors is essential, under the leadership of your bishops, for deepening, proclaiming and effectively promoting the truth about man, his dignity and his inalienable rights, the truth such as the Church receives it in revelation and such as she ceaselessly develops it in her social teaching in the light of the Gospel. These shared convictions, however, are not a ready-made model for society (cf. *Octogesima Adveniens,* 42). It is principally the task of lay people to put them into practice in concrete projects, to define priorities and to develop models that are suitable for promoting man's real good. The Second Vatican Council's pastoral constitution *Gaudium et Spes,* tells us that "lay people should seek from priests light and spiritual strength. Let the people not imagine that their pastors are always such experts, that to every

problem which arises, however complicated, they can readily give a concrete solution, or even that such is their mission. Rather, enlightened by Christian wisdom and giving close attention to the teaching authority of the church, let the lay people assume their own distinctive role" (*Gaudium et Spes,* 43).

The frenzy of consumerism

6. In order to bring this undertaking to a successful conclusion, fresh spiritual and moral energy drawn from the inexhaustible divine source is needed. This energy does not develop easily. The lifestyle of many members of our rich and permissive societies is easy, and so is the lifestyle of increasing groups inside the poorer countries. As I said last year to the plenary assembly of the Pontifical Commission Justice and Peace, "Christians will want to be in the vanguard in favoring ways of life that decisively break with the frenzy of consumerism, exhausting and joyless" (Nov. 11, 1978). It is not a question of slowing down progress, for there is no human progress when everything conspires to give full reign to the instincts of self-interest, sex and power. We must find a simple way of living. For it is not right that the standard of living of the rich countries should seek to maintain itself by draining off a great part of the reserves of energy and raw materials that are meant to serve the whole of humanity. For readiness to create a greater and more equitable solidarity between peoples is the first condition for peace.

Catholics of the United States, and all you citizens of

the United States, you have such a tradition of spiritual generosity, industry, simplicity and sacrifice that you cannot fail to heed this call today for a new enthusiasm and a fresh determination.

It is in the joyful simplicity of a life inspired by the Gospel and the Gospel's spirit of fraternal sharing that you will find the best remedy for sour criticism, paralyzing doubt and the temptation to make money the principal means and indeed the very measure of advancement.

7. On various occasions, I have referred to the gospel parable of the rich man and Lazarus. "Once there was a rich man who dressed in purple and linen and feasted splendidly every day. At his gate lay a beggar named Lazarus who was covered with sores. Lazarus longed to eat the scraps that fell from the rich man's table" (Lk. 16:19). Both the rich man and the beggar died and were carried before Abraham, and there judgment was rendered on their conduct. And the scripture tells us that Lazarus found consolation, but that the rich man found torment. Was the rich man condemned because he had riches, because he abounded in earthly possessions, because he "dressed in purple linen and feasted splendidly every day?" No, I would say that it was not for this reason. The rich man was condemned because he did not pay attention to the other man. Because he failed to take notice of Lazarus, the person who sat at his door and who longed to eat the scraps from his table. Nowhere does Christ condemn the mere possession of earthly goods as such. Instead, he pronounces very harsh words against those who use their possessions in a selfish way, without paying attention to the needs of others. The

51

Sermon on the Mount begins with the words: "Blessed are the poor in spirit." And at the end of the account of the Last Judgment as found in St. Matthew's Gospel, Jesus speaks the words that we all know well: "I was hungry and you gave me no food, I was thirsty and you gave me no drink. I was away from home and you gave me no welcome, naked and you gave me no clothing. I was ill and in prison and you did not come and comfort me" (Mt. 25:42-43).

The parable of the rich man and Lazarus must always be present in our memory; it must form our conscience. Christ demands openness from the rich, the affluent, the economically advanced; openness to the poor, the underdeveloped and the disadvantaged. Christ demands an openness that is more than benign attention, more than token actions or half-hearted efforts that leave the poor as destitute as before or even more so.

All of humanity must think of the parable of the rich man and the beggar. Humanity must translate it into contemporary terms of economy and politics, in terms of all human rights, in terms of relations between the First, Second and Third Worlds. We cannot stand idly by when thousands of human beings are dying of hunger. Nor can we remain indifferent when the rights of the human spirit are trampled upon, when violence is done to the human conscience in matters of truth, religion and cultural creativity.

We cannot stand idly by, enjoying our own riches and freedom if, in any place, the Lazarus of the 20th century stands at our doors. In the light of the parable of Christ, riches and freedom mean a special responsibility. Riches and freedom create a special obligation. And so, in the name of the solidarity that binds all together in a common humanity, I again proclaim the dignity of every human person; the rich man and Lazarus are both human beings, both of them equally created in the image and likeness of God, both of them equally redeemed by Christ, at a great price, the price of "the precious blood of Christ" (1 Pt. 1:19).

8. Brothers and sisters in Christ, with deep conviction and affection I repeat to you the words that I addressed to the world when I took up my apostolic ministry in the service of all men and women: "Do not be afraid. Open wide the doors for Christ. To his saving power open the boundaries of states, economic and political systems, the vast fields of culture, civilization and development. Do not be afraid. Christ knows what is in man; he alone knows it" (October 22, 1978).

As I said to you at the beginning, Christ is our justice and our peace, and all our works of justice and peace draw from this source the irreplaceable energy and light for the great task before us. As we resolutely commit ourselves to the service of all the needs of the individuals and of the peoples—for Christ urges us to do so—we shall nevertheless remind ourselves that the Church's mission is not limited to this witness to social fruitfulness of the Gospel. Along this road that leads the Church to man, she does not offer, in the matter of justice and peace, only the earthly fruits of the Gospel; she brings to man—to every person—their very source: Jesus Christ himself, our justice and our peace.

We are an Easter People

Address at St. Charles Borromeo Church in Harlem, October 2.

Dear friends, dear brothers and sisters in Christ,

"This is the day the Lord has made; let us be glad and rejoice in it" (Ps. 118:24).

I greet you in the joy and peace of our Lord Jesus Christ. I welcome this opportunity to be with you and to speak to you, and through you to extend my greetings to all black Americans.

At Cardinal Cooke's suggestion, I was happy to include in my plans a visit to the Parish of Saint Charles Borromeo in Harlem, and to its black community, which for half a century has nurtured here the cultural, social and religious roots of black people. I have greatly looked forward to being here this evening.

I come to you as a servant of Jesus Christ, and I want to speak to you about him. Christ came to bring joy: joy to children, joy to parents, joy to families and to friends, joy to workers and to scholars, joy to the sick and to the elderly, joy to all humanity. In a true sense joy is the keynote of the Christian message and the recurring motif of the Gospels. Recall the first words of the angel to Mary: "Rejoice, O full of grace the Lord is with you" (Lk. 1:28). And at the birth of Jesus, the angels announced to the shepherds: "Listen, I bring you news of great joy, joy to be shared by all people" (Lk. 2:10). Years later as Jesus entered Jerusalem riding on a colt, "the whole group of disciples joyfully began to praise God at the top of their voices. 'Blessed is the King who comes in the name of the Lord'!" (Lk. 19:37-38). We are told that some Pharisees in the crowd complained, saying: "Master, stop your disciples." But Jesus answered: "I tell you, if they were silent, the very stones would cry out" (Lk. 19:39-40).

Are not those words of Jesus still true today? If we are silent about the joy that comes from knowing Jesus, the very stones of our cities will cry out! For we are an Easter people and "Alleluia" is our song. With Saint Paul I exhort you: "Rejoice in the Lord always, I say it again, rejoice" (Phil. 4:4).

Rejoice because Jesus has come into the world!

Rejoice because Jesus has died upon the cross!

Rejoice because he rose again from the dead!

Rejoice because in baptism, he washed away our sins!

Rejoice because Jesus has come to set us free!

And rejoice because he is the master of our life!

But how many people have never known this joy? They feed on emptiness and tread the paths of despair. "They walk in darkness and the shadow of death" (Lk. 1:79). And we need not look to the far ends of the earth for them. They live in our neighborhoods, they walk down our streets, they may even be members of our own families. They live without true joy because they live without hope. They live without hope because they have never heard, really heard the Good News of Jesus Christ, because they have never met a brother or a sister who touched their lives with the love of Jesus and lifted them up from their misery.

We must go to them therefore as messengers of hope. We must bring to them the witness of true joy. We must pledge to them our commitment to work for a just society and city where they feel respected and loved.

And so I encourage you, be men and women of deep and abiding faith. Be heralds of hope. Be messengers of joy. Be true workers for justice. Let the Good News of Christ radiate from your hearts, and the peace he alone gives remain forever in your souls.

My dear brothers and sisters in the black community: "Rejoice in the Lord always, again I say rejoice."

Look to Christ

Address to students at Madison Square Garden,
New York City, October 3.

Dear young people,

1. I am happy to be with you in Madison Square Garden. Today this is a garden of life, where young people are alive: alive with hope and love, alive with the life of Christ. And it is in the name of Christ that I greet each one of you today.

I have been told that most of you come from Catholic high schools. For this reason I would like to say something about Catholic education, to tell you why the church considers it so important and expends so much energy in order to provide you and millions of other young people with a Catholic education. The answer can be summarized in one word, in one person, Jesus Christ. The church wants to communicate Christ to you.

This is what education is all about, this is the meaning of life: to know Christ. To know Christ as a friend, as someone who cares about you and the person next to you, and all the people here and everywhere—no matter what language they speak, or what clothes they wear, or what color their skin is.

And so the purpose of Catholic education is to communicate Christ to you, so that your attitude toward others will be that of Christ. You are approaching that stage in your life when you must take personal responsibility for your own destiny. Soon you will be making major decisions which will affect the whole course of your life. If these decisions reflect Christ's attitude, then your education will be a success.

Learn to meet challenges

We have to learn to meet challenges and even crises in the light of Christ's cross and resurrection. Part of our Catholic education is to learn to see the needs of others, to have the courage to practice what we believe in. With the support of a Catholic education we try to meet every circumstance of life with the attitude of Christ. Yes, the church wants to communicate Christ to you so that you will come to full maturity in him who is the perfect human being, and at the same time, the Son of God.

2. Dear young people: you and I and all of us together make up the Church, and we are convinced that only in Christ do we find real love and the fullness of life.

And so I invite you today to look to Christ.

When you wonder about the mystery of yourself, look to Christ who gives you the meaning of life.

When you wonder what it means to be a mature person, look to Christ who is the fullness of humanity.

And when you wonder about your role in the future of the world and of the United States, look to Christ. Only in Christ will you fulfill your potential as an American

Responding to the 19,000 exultant youths in Madison Square Garden who roared their welcome, the Pope waves his arms in a gesture of recognition to the young people's sense of vitality.

citizen and as a citizen of the world community.

3. With the aid of your Catholic education, you have received the greatest of gifts: "I believe nothing can happen that will outweigh the supreme advantage of knowing Christ Jesus my Lord. For him I have accepted the loss of everything and I look on everything as so much rubbish if only I can have Christ and be given a place in him" (Phil. 3:8-9).

Gratitude and responsibility

Be always grateful to God for this gift of knowing Christ. Be grateful also to your parents and to the community of the Church for making possible, through many sacrifices, your Catholic education. People have placed a lot of hope in you and they now look forward to your collaboration in giving witness to Christ, and in transmitting the Gospel to others. The Church needs you. The world needs you, because it needs Christ, and you belong to Christ. And so I ask you to accept your responsibility in the Church, the responsibility of your Catholic education: to help—by your words and, above all, by the example of your lives—to spread the Gospel. You do this by praying and by being just and truthful and pure.

Dear young people: By a real Christian life, by the practice of your religion you are called to give witness to your faith. And because actions speak louder than words, you are called to proclaim, by the conduct of your daily lives that you really do believe that Jesus Christ is Lord!

A Symbol of Freedom

Address at Battery Park, New York City, October 3.

Dear friends of New York,

1. My visit to your city would not have been complete without coming to Battery Park, without seeing Ellis Island and the Statue of Liberty in the distance. Every nation has its historical symbols. They may be shrines or statues or documents; but their significance lies in the truths they represent to the citizens of a nation and in the image they convey to other nations. Such a symbol in the United States is the Statue of Liberty. This is an impressive symbol of what the United States has stood for from the very beginning of its history; *this is a symbol of freedom.* It reflects the immigrant history of the United States, for it was freedom that millions of human beings were looking for on these shores. And it was freedom that the young republic offered in compassion. On this spot, I wish to pay homage to this noble trait of America and its people: its desire to be free, its determination to preserve freedom, and its willingness to share this freedom with others. May the ideal of liberty, of freedom, remain

a moving force for your nation and for all the nations in the world today!

2. It greatly honors your country and its citizens that on this foundation of liberty you have built a nation where the dignity of every human person is to be respected, where a religious sense and a strong family structure are fostered, where duty and honest work are held in high esteem, where generosity and hospitality are no idle words, and where the right to religious liberty is deeply rooted in your history.

Yesterday, before the General Assembly of the United Nations, I made a plea for peace and justice based on the full respect for all the fundamental rights of the human person. I also spoke of religious freedom because it regards a person's relationship to God, and because it is related in a special way to other human rights. It is closely allied with the right to freedom of conscience. If conscience is not secure in society, then the security of all other rights is threatened.

Freedom and truth

Liberty, in all its aspects, must be based on truth. I want to repeat here the words of Jesus "the truth will make you free" (Jn. 8:32). It is, then, my wish that your sense of freedom may always go hand in hand with a profound sense of truth and honesty about yourselves and about the realities of your society. Past achievements can never be an acceptable substitute for present responsibilities toward the common good of the society you live in and towards your fellow citizens. Just as the desire for freedom is a universal aspiration in the world today, so is the quest for justice. No institution or organization can credibly stand for freedom today if it does not also support the quest for justice, for both are essential demands of the human spirit.

3. It will always remain one of the glorious achievements of this nation that, when people looked toward America, they received together with freedom also a chance for their own advancement. This tradition must be honored also today. The freedom that was gained must be ratified each day by the firm rejection of whatever wounds, weakens or dishonors human life. And so I appeal to all who love freedom and justice to give a chance to all in need, to the poor and the powerless. Break open the hopeless cycles of poverty and ignorance that are still the lot of too many of our brothers and sisters; the hopeless cycles of prejudice that linger on despite enormous progress toward effective equality in education and employment; the cycles of despair in which are imprisoned all those that lack decent food, shelter or employment; the cycles of underdevelopment that are the consequence of international mechanisms that subordinate human existence to the domination of partially conceived economic progress; and finally the inhuman cycle of war that springs from the violation of man's fundamental rights and produces still graver violations of them.

Freedom in justice

Freedom in justice will bring a new dawn of hope for the present generation as it has done before: for the homeless, for the unemployed, for the aging, for the sick and the handicapped, for the migrants and the undocumented workers, for all who hunger for human dignity in this land and in the world.

4. With sentiments of admiration and with confidence in your potential for true human greatness, I wish to greet in you the rich variety of your nation, where people of different ethnic origins and creeds can live, work and prosper together in freedom and mutual respect. I greet and I thank for their cordial welcome all those who joined me here: businessmen and laborers, scholars and managers, social workers and civil servants, old and young, I greet you with respect, esteem and love. My warm greetings go to each and every group. To my fellow Catholics, to the members of the different Christian churches with whom I am united in faith in Jesus Christ.

And I address a special word of greeting to the leaders of the Jewish community whose presence here honors me greatly. A few months ago, I met with an international group of Jewish representatives in Rome. On that occasion, recalling the initiatives undertaken following the Second Vatican Council under my predecessor Paul VI, I stated that "our two communities are connected and closely related at the very level of their respective religious identities," and that, on this basis, "we recognize with utmost clarity that the path along which we should proceed is one of fraternal dialogue and fruitful collaboration" (*L'Osservatore Romano,* March 12-13, 1979). I am glad to ascertain that this same path has been followed here, in the United States, by large sections of both communities and their respective authorities and representatives bodies. Several common programs of study, mutual knowledge, a common determination to reject all forms of anti-Semitism and discrimination, and various forms of collaboration for human advancement, inspired by our common biblical heritage, have created deep and permanent links between Jews and Catholics. As one who in my homeland has shared the suffering of your brethren. I greet you with the word taken from the Hebrew language: Shalom! Peace be with you.

And to everyone here I offer the expression of my respect, my esteem and my fraternal love. May God bless all of you! May God bless New York!

A City Needs a Soul

Address at Shea Stadium, New York City, October 3.

Dear friends in New York,

It gives me great joy to have the opportunity to come and greet you on my way to La Guardia Airport, at the end of my visit to the archdiocese and to the metropolis of New York.

Thank you for your warm welcome. In you I wish to greet once again all the people of New York: all your parishes, hospitals, schools and organizations, your sick and aged. And with special affection I greet the young people and the children.

From Rome I bring you a message of faith and love. "May the peace of Christ reign in your hearts!" (Col. 3:15). Make peace the desire of your heart, for if you love peace, you will love all humanity, without distinction of race, color or creed.

My greeting is also an invitation to all of you to feel personally responsible for the well-being and the community spirit of your city. A visitor to New York is always impressed by the special character of this metropolis: skyscrapers, endless streets, large residential areas, housing blocks, and above all the millions of people who live here or who look here for the work that will sustain them and their family.

Large concentrations of people create special problems and special needs. The personal effort and loyal collaboration of everybody are needed to find the right solutions, so that all men, women and children can live in dignity and develop to the full their potential without having to suffer for lack of education, housing, employment, and cultural opportunities. Above all, a city needs a soul if it is to become a true home for human beings. You, the people, must give it this soul. And how do you do this? By loving each other. Love for each other must be the hallmark of your lives. In the Gospel Jesus Christ tells us: "You shall love your neighbor as yourself" (Mt. 22:39). This commandment of the Lord must be your inspiration in forming true human relationships among yourselves, so that nobody will ever feel alone or unwanted, or much less, rejected, despised or hated. Jesus himself will give you the power of fraternal love. And every neighborhood, every block, every street will become a true community because you will want it so, and Jesus will help you to bring it about.

Keep Christ in your hearts

Keep Jesus Christ in your hearts, and you will recognize his face in every human being. You will want to help him out in all his needs: the needs of your brothers and sisters. This is the way we prepare ourselves to meet Jesus, when he will come again, on the last day, as the judge of the living and the dead, and he will say to us: "Come, you have my Father's blessing! Inherit the kingdom prepared for you from the creation of the world. For I was hungry and you gave me food, I was thirsty and you gave me drink. I was a stranger and you welcomed me, naked and you clothed me. I was ill and you comforted me, in prison and you came to visit me... I assure you as often as you did it for one of my least brethren, you did it for me" (Mt. 25:34-35, 39).

I now wish to address a very cordial welcome to each and every member of the Spanish-speaking colony, coming from various countries, here in this stadium.

In you, I see and I wish to greet, with great affection, the whole of the numerous Hispanic community living in New York and many other places in the United States.

I wish to assure you that I am well aware of the place that you occupy in American society, and that I follow with lively interest your accomplishments, aspirations and difficulties within the social fabric of this nation, which is your homeland of adoption or the land that welcomes you. For this reason, from the very moment that I accepted the invitation to visit this country, I thought of you, who are an integral and specific part of this society, a very considerable part of the Church in this vast nation.

I wish to exhort you as Catholics, always to maintain very clearly your Christian identity, with a constant reference to the values of your faith, values that must enlighten the legitimate quest for a worthy material position for yourselves and your families.

Since you are generally immersed in the environment of heavily populated cities and in a social climate where sometimes technology and material values take first place, make an effort to provide a spiritual contribution to your life and your neighborhood. Keep close to God in your lives, to the God who calls you to be ever more worthy of your condition as human beings with an eternal vocation, to the God who invites you to solidarity and to collaboration in building up an ever more human, just and fraternal world.

I pray for you, for your families and friends, above all for your children, for the sick and suffering, and to all of you I give my blessing. May God be with you always!

Good-bye, and God bless you.

PHILADELPHIA

C. Slattery

The Holy Father waves to some of the million or so Philadelphians who attended the Mass in Logan Square where, in his homily, Pope John Paul II returned to the theme of freedom in relation to the message of Jesus Christ.

God's Law:

The Standard of Liberty

*Homily of the Mass at Logan Circle in Philadelphia,
October 3.*

Dear brothers and sisters of the Church in Philadelphia.

1. It is a great joy for me to celebrate the Eucharist
with you today. All of us are gathered together as one
community, one people in the grace and peace of God
our Father and of the Lord Jesus Christ. We are gathered
in the fellowship of the Holy Spirit. We have come
together to proclaim the Gospel in all its power, for the
Eucharistic sacrifice is the summit and enactment of our
proclamation:

Christ has died, Christ is risen, Christ will come again!

From this altar of sacrifice, there arises a hymn of
praise and thanksgiving to God through Jesus Christ. We
who belong to Christ are all part of this hymn, this
sacrifice of praise. The sacrifice of Calvary is renewed
on this altar and it becomes our offering too—an offering
for the benefit of the living and the dead, an offering for
the universal Church.

Assembled in the charity of Christ, we are all one in his sacrifice:

- the cardinal archbishop who is called to lead this church in the path of truth and love;
- his auxiliary bishops and the diocesan and religious clergy, who share with bishops in the preaching of the word;
- men and women religious, who through the consecration of their lives show the world what it means to be faithful to the message of the Beatitudes;
- fathers and mothers, with their great mission of building up the Church in love;
- every category of the laity with their particular task in the Church's mission of evangelization and salvation.

This sacrifice offered today in Philadelphia is the expression of our praying community. In union with Jesus Christ we make intercession for the universal Church, for the well-being of all our fellow men and women, and, today in particular, for the preservation of all the human and Christian values that are the heritage of this land, this country and this very city.

2. Philadelphia is the city of the Declaration of Independence, that remarkable document containing a solemn attestation of the equality of all human beings endowed by their Creator with certain inalienable rights: life, liberty and the pursuit of happiness, expressing a "firm reliance on the protection of Divine Providence." These are the sound moral principles formulated by our founding fathers and enshrined forever in your history.

In the human and civil values that are contained in the spirit of this Declaration there are easily recognized strong connections with basic religious and Christian values. A sense of religion itself is part of this heritage. The Liberty Bell which I visited on another occasion proudly bears the words of the Bible: "Proclaim liberty throughout the land" (Lv. 25:10). This tradition poses for all future generations of America a noble challenge: "One nation under God, indivisible, with liberty and justice for all."

Human and Christian Values

3. As citizens, you must strive to preserve these human values, to understand them better and to define their consequences for the whole community and as a worthy contribution to the world. As Christians, you must strengthen these human values and complement them by confronting them with the gospel message, so that you may discover their deeper meaning, and thus assume more fully your duties and obligations toward your fellow human beings, with whom you are bound in a common destiny. In a way, for us who know Jesus Christ, human and Christian values are but two aspects of the same reality: the reality of man, redeemed by Christ and called to the fullness of eternal life.

In my first encyclical letter, I stated this important truth: "Christ, the Redeemer of the world, is the one who penetrated in a unique unrepeatable way into the mystery of man and entered his 'heart.' Rightly therefore does Second Vatican Council teach: 'The truth is that only in the mystery of the Incarnate Word does the mystery of man take on light. For Adam, the first man, was a type of him who was to come (Rom. 5:14), Christ the Lord. Christ the new Adam, in the very revelation of the mystery of the Father and his love, fully reveals man to himself and brings to light his most high calling' '' (*Redemptor Hominis,* 8). It is then in Jesus Christ that every man, woman and child is called to find the answer to the questions regarding the values that will inspire his or her personal and social relations.

4. How then can a Christian, inspired and guided by the mystery of the incarnation and redemption of Christ, strengthen his or her own values and those that are embodied in the heritage of this nation? The answer to that question, in order to be complete, would have to be long. Let me, however, just touch upon a few important points.

These values are strengthened when power and authority are exercised in full respect for all the fundamental rights of the human person, whose dignity is the dignity of one created in the image and likeness of God (Gn. 1:26); when freedom is accepted, not as an absolute end in itself, but as a gift that enables self-giving and service; when the family is protected and strengthened; when its unity is preserved, and when its role as the basic cell of society is recognized and honored.

Human-Christian values are fostered when every effort is made so that no child anywhere in the world faces death because of lack of food, or faces a diminished intellectual and physical potential for want of sufficient nourishment, or has to bear all through life the scars of deprivation.

Human-Christian values triumph when any system is

reformed that authorizes the exploitation of any human being; when upright service and honesty in public servants is promoted; when the dispensing of justice is fair and the same for all; when responsible use is made of the material and energy resources of the world—resources that are meant for the benefit of all; when the environment is preserved intact for the future generations.

Human-Christian values triumph by subjecting political and economic considerations to human dignity, by making them serve the cause of man—every person created by God, every brother and sister redeemed by Christ.

Freedom and the moral good

5. I have mentioned the Declaration of Independence and the Liberty Bell, two monuments that exemplify the spirit of freedom on which this country was founded. Your attachment to liberty, to freedom, is part of your heritage. When the Liberty Bell rang for the first time in 1776, it was to announce the freedom of your nation, the beginning of the pursuit of a common destiny independent of any outside coercion. This principle of freedom is paramount in the political and social order, in relationships between the government and the people, and between individual and individual.

However, man's life is also lived in another order of reality: the order of his relationship to what is objectively true and morally good. Freedom thus acquires a deeper meaning when it is referred to the human person. It concerns in the first place the relation of man to himself. Every human person, endowed with reason, is free when he is the master of his own actions, when he is capable of choosing that good which is in conformity with reason, and therefore with his own human dignity.

Freedom can never tolerate an offense against the rights of others, and one of the fundamental rights of man is the right to worship God. In the Declaration on Religious Freedom, the Second Vatican Council stated that the "demand for freedom in human society chiefly regards the quest for the values proper to the human spirit. It regards in the first place the free exercise of religion in society... Religious freedom, which men demand as necessary to fulfill their duty to worship God, has to do with immunity from coercion in civil society. Therefore it leaves untouched traditional Catholic teaching on the moral duty of men and societies toward the true religion and toward the one Church of Christ" (*Dignitatis Humanae.* 1).

Freedom and truth

6. Christ himself linked freedom with the knowledge of truth. "You will know the truth and the truth will make you free" (Jn. 8:32).

In my first encyclical, I wrote in this regard: "These words contain both a fundamental requirement and a warning: the requirement of an honest relationship with regard to truth as a condition for authentic freedom, and the warning to avoid every kind of illusory freedom, every superficial unilateral freedom, every freedom that fails to enter into the whole truth about man and the world" (*Redemptor Hominis,* 12).

Freedom can therefore never be construed without relation to the truth as revealed by Jesus Christ and proposed by his Church, nor can it be seen as a pretext for moral anarchy, for every moral order must remain linked to truth. St. Peter, in his first letter, says: "Live as free men, but do not use your freedom for malice" (1 Pt. 2:16). No freedom can exist when it goes against man in what he is or against man in his relationship to others and to God.

This is especially relevant when one considers the domain of human sexuality. Here, as in any other field, there can be no true freedom without respect for the truth regarding the nature of human sexuality and marriage.

In today's society, we see so many disturbing tendencies and so much laxity regarding the Christian view on sexuality that have all one thing in common: recourse to the concept of freedom to justify any behavior that is no longer consonant with the true moral order and the teaching of the Church. Moral norms do not militate against the freedom of the person or the couple. On the contrary, they exist precisely for that freedom, since they are given to ensure the right use of freedom. Whoever refuses to accept these norms and to act accordingly, whoever seeks to liberate himself or herself from these norms, is not truly free.

Free indeed is the person who models his or her behavior in a responsible way according to the exigencies of the objective good. What I have said here regards the whole of conjugal morality, but it applies as well to the priests with regard to the obligations of celibacy. The cohesion of freedom and ethics has also its consequences for the pursuit of the common good in society and for the national independence which the Liberty Bell announced two centuries ago.

7. Divine law is the sole standard of human liberty and is given to us in the Gospel of Christ, the Gospel of redemption. But fidelity to this Gospel of redemption will never be possible without the action of the Holy Spirit. It is the Holy Spirit who guards the life-giving message entrusted to the Church. It is the Holy Spirit who ensures the faithful transmission of the Gospel into the lives of all of us. It is by the action of the Holy Spirit that the Church is built up day after day into a kingdom: a kingdom of truth and life, a kingdom of holiness and grace, a universal kingdom of justice, love and peace.

Today, therefore, we come before the Father to offer him the petitions and desires of our hearts, to offer him praise and thanksgiving. We do this from the city of Philadelphia for the universal Church and for the world. We do this as "members of the household of God" (Eph. 2:19) in union with the sacrifice of Christ Jesus, our cornerstone, for the glory of the most Holy Trinity. Amen.

Perseverance
Through Prayer

Address to seminarians at Overbrook, Pennsylvania,
October 3.

Beloved brothers and sons in Christ,

One of the things I wanted most to do during my visit
to the United States has now arrived. I wanted to visit a
seminary and meet the seminarians; and through you I
would like to communicate to all seminarians how much
you mean to me, and how much you mean for the future
of the Church—for the future of the mission given to us
by Christ.

You hold a special place in my thoughts and prayers.
In your lives there is great promise for the future of
evangelization. And you give us hope that the authentic
renewal of the Church which was begun by the Second
Vatican Council will be brought to fruition. But in order
for this to happen, you must receive a solid and well-
rounded preparation in the seminary. This personal
conviction about the importance of seminaries prompted
me to write these words in my Holy Thursday letter to the
bishops of the Church:

"The full reconstitution of the life of the seminaries

throughout the church will be the best proof of the achievement of the renewal to which the Council directed the Church."

If seminaries are to fulfill their mission in the Church two activities in the overall program of the seminary are crucially important: the teaching of God's word, and discipline.

God's word and discipline

The intellectual formation of the priest, which is so vital for the times in which we live, embraces a number of the human sciences as well as the various sacred sciences. These all have an important place in your preparation for the priesthood. But the first priority for seminaries today is the teaching of God's word in all its purity and integrity, with all its demands and in all its power. This was clearly affirmed by my beloved predecessor Paul VI when he stated that Sacred Scripture is "a perpetual source of spiritual life, the chief instrument for handing down Christian doctrine, and the center of all theological study" (Apostolic Constitution *"Missale Romanum,"* April 3, 1969). Therefore if you, the seminarians of this generation, are to be adequately prepared to take on the heritage and challenge of the Second Vatican Council, you will need to be well trained in the word of God.

Secondly, the seminary must provide a sound discipline to prepare for a life of consecrated service in the image of Christ. Its purpose was well-defined by the Second Vatican Council:

"The discipline required by seminary life should not be

regarded merely as a strong support of community life and of charity. For it is a necessary part of the whole training program designed to provide self-mastery, to foster solid maturity of personality, and to develop other traits of character which are extremely serviceable for the ordered and productive activity of the Church" (*"Optatam Totius,"* 11).

When discipline is properly exercised, it can create an atmosphere of recollection which enables the seminarian to develop interiorly those attitudes which are so desirable in a priest, such as joyful obedience, generosity and self-sacrifice. In the different forms of community life that are appropriate for the seminary, you will learn the art of dialogue: the capacity to listen to others and to discover the richness of their personality, and the ability to give of yourself. Seminary discipline will reinforce, rather than diminish your freedom, for it will help develop in you those traits and attitudes of mind and heart which God has given you, and which enrich your humanity and help you to serve more effectively his people. Discipline will also assist you in ratifying day after day in your hearts the obedience you owe to Christ and his Church.

The importance of fidelity

I want to remind you of the importance of fidelity. Before you can be ordained, you are called by Christ to make a free and irrevocable commitment to be faithful to him and to his Church. Human dignity requires that you maintain this commitment, that you keep your promise to Christ no matter what difficulties you may encounter, and no matter what temptations you may be exposed to.

The seriousness of this irrevocable commitment places a special obligation upon the rector and faculty of the seminary—and in a particular way on the spiritual director—to help you to evaluate your own suitability for ordination. It is then the responsibility of the bishop to judge whether you should be called to the priesthood.

It is important that one's commitment be made with full awareness and personal freedom. And so, during these years in the seminary, take time to reflect on the serious obligations and the difficulties which are part of the priest's life. Consider whether Christ is calling you to the celibate life. You can make a responsible decision for celibacy only after you have reached the firm conviction that Christ is indeed offering you this gift, which is intended for the good of the Church and for the service of others (cf. *Letter to Priests,* 9).

Men of prayer

To understand what it means to be faithful we must look to Christ, the "faithful witness" (Rev. 1:5), the Son who "learned to obey through what he suffered" (Heb. 5:8); to Jesus who said: "My aim is to do not my own will, but the will of him who sent me" (Jn. 5:30). We look to Jesus, not only to see and contemplate his fidelity to the Father despite all opposition (cf. Heb. 23:3), but also to learn from him the means he employed in order to be faithful: especially prayer and abandonment to God's will (cf. Lk. 22:39).

Remember that in the final analysis perseverance in

fidelity is a proof, not of human strength and courage, but of the efficacy of Christ's grace. And so if we are going to persevere we shall have to be men of prayer who, through the Eucharist, the Liturgy of the Hours and our personal encounters with Christ, find the courage and grace to be faithful. Let us be confident then, remembering the words of St. Paul: "There is nothing that I cannot master with the help of the one who gives me strength" (Phil. 4:13).

My brothers and sons in Christ, keep in mind the priorities of the priesthood to which you aspire: namely prayer and the ministry of the word (Acts 6:4).

"It is prayer that shows the essential style of the priest; without prayer this style becomes deformed. Prayer helps us always to find the light that has led us since the beginning of our priestly vocation, and which never ceases to lead us... Prayer enables us to be converted continually, to remain in a state of continuous reaching out to God, which is essential if we wish to lead others to him. Prayer helps us to believe, to hope and to love." (*Letter to Priests,* 10).

It is my hope that during your years in the seminary you will develop an ever greater hunger for the word of God (cf. Amos 8:11). Meditate on this word daily and study it continually, so that your whole life may become a proclamation of Christ, the word made flesh (cf. Jn. 1:14). In this word of God are the beginning and end of all ministry, the purpose of all pastoral activity, the rejuvenating source for faithful perseverance and the one thing which can give meaning and unity to the varied activities of a priest.

"Let the message of Christ, in all its richness, find a home with you" (Col. 3:16). In the knowledge of Christ you have the key to the Gospel. In the knowledge of Christ you have an understanding of the needs of the world. Since he became one with us in all things but sin, your union with Jesus of Nazareth could never, and will never be an obstacle to understanding and responding to the needs of the world. And finally, in the knowledge of Christ, you will not only discover, and come to understand, the limitations of human wisdom and of human solutions to the needs of humanity, but you will also experience the power of Jesus, and the value of human reason and human endeavor when they are taken up in the strength of Jesus, when they are redeemed in Christ.

May Our Blessed Mother Mary protect you today and always.

May I also take this opportunity to greet the lay people who are present today at St. Charles Seminary. Your presence here is a sign of your esteem for the ministerial priesthood, as well as being a reminder of that close cooperation between laity and priests which is needed if the mission of Christ is to be fulfilled in our time. I am happy that you are present and I am grateful for all that you do for the church in Philadelphia. In particular I ask you to pray for these young men, and for all seminarians that they may persevere in their calling. Please pray for all priests and for the success of their ministry among God's people. And please pray the Lord of the harvest to send more laborers into his vineyard, the Church.

Unity and Charity

Address to Ukrainian Catholics in Philadelphia,
October 4.

Dear brothers and sisters,

"Now in Christ Jesus...you are citizens like all the saints, and part of God's household. You are part of a building that has the apostles and prophets for its foundations, and Christ Jesus himself for its main cornerstone" (Eph. 2:23, 19-20). With these words the Apostle Paul reminded the Ephesians of the tremendous blessing they had received in becoming members of the Church. And those words are still true today. You are part of the household of God. You, members of the Ukrainian tradition, are part of a building that has the apostles and prophets for its foundations, and Christ Jesus himself for its main cornerstone. This has all occurred according to the providential plan of God.

Several years ago, my beloved predecessor, Paul VI, gave a stone from the tomb of St. Peter to be included in the construction of this beautiful cathedral dedicated to Mary Immaculate. Pope Paul intended this gift to be a visible symbol of the love and esteem of the Apostolic See of Rome for the Ukrainian church. At the same time, this stone was meant to serve as a sign of the fidelity of the Ukrainian church to the See of Peter. In this profound symbolic gesture, Paul VI was reaffirming the teaching of the apostle Paul in the letter to the Ephesians.

Today, as successor to Paul VI in the chair of St. Peter, I come to visit you in this magnificent new cathedral. I am happy for this opportunity. I welcome the occasion to assure you, as universal pastor of the Church, that all who have inherited the Ukrainian tradition have an important and distinguished part to fulfill in the Catholic Church.

As history testifies, the Church developed a number of rites and traditions as in the course of time she spread from Jerusalem to the nations and took flesh in the language, culture and human traditions of the individual peoples who accepted the Gospel with open hearts. These various rites and traditions, far from being a sign of deviation, infidelity or disunity, were in fact unfailing proof of the presence of the Holy Spirit who continually renews and enriches the Church, the kingdom of Christ already present in mystery (cf. *Lumen Gentium,* 3).

The heritage of the Church

The various traditions within the Church give expression to the multitude of ways the Gospel can take root and flower in the lives of God's people. They are living evidence of the richness of the Church. Each one, while united to all the others in the "same faith, the same sacraments and the same government" (*"Orientalium*

Ecclesiarum," 2), is nevertheless manifested in its own liturgy, ecclesiastical discipline and spiritual patrimony. Each tradition combined particular insights with an unparalleled lived experience of being faithful to Christ. It was in view of these considerations that the Second Vatican Council declared: "History, tradition and numerous ecclesiastical institutions clearly manifest how much the universal Church is indebted to the Eastern churches. Thus this sacred synod not only honors this ecclesiastical and spiritual heritage with merited esteem and rightful praise, but also unhesitatingly looks upon it as the heritage of Christ's universal Church" (*Orientalium Ecclesiarum,* 5).

For many years, I have highly esteemed the Ukrainian people. I have known of the many sufferings and injustices you have endured. These have been and continue to be matters of great concern to me. I am also mindful of the struggles of the Ukrainian Catholic Church, throughout its history, to remain faithful to the Gospel and to be in union with the successor of St. Peter. I cannot forget the countless Ukrainian martyrs, in ancient and more recent times, most of whose names are unknown, who gave up their lives rather than abandon their faith. I mention these in order to show my profound esteem for the Ukrainian church and its proved fidelity in suffering.

I also wish to mention those things which you have preserved as your special patrimony: the Slavonic liturgical language, the ecclesiastical music and the numerous forms of piety which have developed over the centuries and continue to nourish your lives. Your appreciation of these treasures of the Ukrainian tradition is demonstrated by the way that you have maintained your attachment with the Ukrainian church and have continued to live the faith according to its unique tradition.

My brothers and sisters in Christ, I want to recall in your presence the words Jesus prayed on the vigil of his death upon the cross: "Father...that they may be one" (Jn. 17:11). We must never forget this prayer; in fact we must continually search for still better ways to safeguard and strengthen the bonds of union which unite us in the one Catholic Church.

Unity of doctrine

Remember the words of St. Paul: "You form part of a building that has the apostles and prophets for its foundations, and Christ himself for its main cornerstone" (Eph. 2:20). The unity of this spiritual building, which is the Church, is preserved by fidelity to the cornerstone, who is Christ, and to the teaching of the apostles preserved and explained in the tradition of the Church. A real unity of doctrine binds us as one.

Catholic unity also entails a recognition of the successor of St. Peter and his ministry of strengthening and preserving intact the communion of the universal Church, while safeguarding the existence of legitimate individual traditions within it. The Ukrainian church, as well as the other Eastern churches, has a right and duty, in accordance with the teaching of the council (cf. *"Orientalium Ecclesiarum,"* 5), to preserve its own ecclesiastical and spiritual patrimony. It is precisely because these individual traditions are also intended for the enrichment of the universal Church that the Apostolic See of Rome takes great care to protect and foster each one. In turn, the ecclesial communities that follow these traditions are called to adhere with love and respect to certain particular forms of discipline which my predecessors and I, in fulfilling our pastoral responsibility to the universal Church, have judged necessary for the well-being of the whole body of Christ.

To a great extent, our Catholic unity depends on mutual charity. Let us remember that the unity of the Church originated on the cross of Christ, which broke down the barriers of sin and division and reconciled us with God and one another. Jesus foretold this unifying act when he said: "...and I, if I be lifted up from the earth, will draw all men to myself" (Jn. 12:32). If we continue to imitate the love of Jesus, our Savior, on the cross, and if we persevere in love for one another, then we shall preserve the bonds of unity in the Church and witness the fulfillment of Jesus's prayer: "Father...that they may be one" (Jn. 17:11).

Filial love for Mary

As for the future, I entrust you to the protection of Mary Immaculate, the mother of God, the mother of the Church. I know that you honor her with great devotion. This magnificent cathedral dedicated to the Immaculate Conception bears eloquent witness to your filial love. And for centuries our Blessed Mother has been the strength of your people throughout their sufferings, and her loving intercession has been a cause of their joy.

Continue to entrust yourselves to her protection.

Continue to be faithful to her Son, our Lord Jesus Christ, the redeemer of the world.

And may the grace of Our Lord Jesus Christ be with you all.

F. Dolan

Leaving the Vatican Observer's residence to return to the UN, the Holy Father receives a gift of flowers from a young boy and girl.

Perfect Self-Giving

Homily to priests at Mass in Philadelphia Civic Center, October 4.

Dear Brother Priests,

1. As we celebrate this Mass, which brings together the presidents or chairmen of the priests' senates, or councils, of all the dioceses of the United States, the theme that suggests itself to our reflection is a vital one: the priesthood itself and its central importance to the task of the Church.

In the encyclical letter *Redemptor Hominis,* I described this task in these words: "The Church's fundamental function in every age and particularly in ours is to direct man's gaze, to point the awareness and experience of the whole of humanity toward the mystery of God, to help men to be familiar with the profundity of the redemption taking place in Christ Jesus" (*Redemptor Hominis,* 10).

Priests' senates are a new structure in the Church, called for by the Second Vatican Council and recent Church legislation. This new structure gives a concrete expression to the unity of bishop and priests in the service of shepherding the flock of Christ, and it assists the bishop in his distinctive role of governing the diocese, by guaranteeing for him the counsel of representative advisers from among the presbyterium.

Our concelebration of today's Eucharist is intended to be a mark of affirmation for the good that has been achieved by your priests' senates during these past years, as well as an encouragement to pursue with enthusiasm and determination this important aim, which is "to bring the life and activity of the people of God into greater conformity with the Gospel" (cf. *Ecclesiae Sanctae* 16:1).

Most of all, however, I want this to be the special occasion on which I can speak through you to all my brother priests throughout this nation about our priesthood. With great love I repeat the words that I wrote to you on Holy Thursday: "For you I am a bishop, with you I am a priest."

A call to service

Our priestly vocation is given by the Lord Jesus himself.

—It is a call which is personal and individual: We are called by name as was Jeremiah.

—It is a call to service: We are sent out to preach the good news, to "give God's flock a shepherd's care."

—It is a call to communion of purpose and of action: to be one priesthood with Jesus and with one another, just as Jesus and his Father are one—a unity so beautifully symbolized in this concelebrated Mass.

Priesthood is not merely a task which has been assigned. It is a vocation, a call to be heard again and again. To hear this call and to respond generously to what this call entails is a task for each priest, but it is also a responsibility for the senates of priests. This responsibility means deepening our understanding of the priesthood as Christ instituted it, as he wanted it to be and to remain, and as the Church faithfully explains it and transmits it.

Fidelity to the call to the priesthood means building up this priesthood with God's people by a life of service according to apostolic priorities: concentration "on prayer and the ministry of the word" (Acts 6:4).

In the Gospel of St. Mark the priestly call of the twelve apostles is like a bud whose flowering displays a whole theology of priesthood. In the midst of Jesus' ministry we read that "he went up the mountain and summoned the men he himself had decided on, who came and joined him. He named twelve as his companions whom he would send to preach the good news..."

The passage then lists the names of the twelve (Mk. 3:13-14). Here we see three significant aspects of the call given by Jesus. He called his first priests individually and by name; he called them for the service of his word, to preach the Gospel; and he made them his own companions, drawing them into that unity of life and action which he shares with his Father in the very life of the Trinity.

2. Let us explore these three dimensions of our priesthood by reflecting on today's scripture readings. For it is in the tradition of the prophetic call that the Gospel places the priestly vocation of the twelve apostles of Jesus.

When the priest reflects on Jeremiah's call to be a prophet he is both reassured and disturbed. "Have no fear...because I am with you to deliver you," says the Lord to the one whom he calls. "For look, I place my words in your mouth."

Who would not take heart at hearing such divine assurance? Yet when we consider why such reassurance is needed, do we not see in ourselves that same reluctance we find in Jeremiah's reply? Like him, at times, our concept of this ministry is too earth-bound; we lack confidence in him who calls us.

It is God who calls

We can also become too attached to our own vision of ministry, thinking that it depends too much on our own talents and abilities, and at times forgetting that it is God who calls us, as he called Jeremiah from the womb. Nor is it our work or our ability that is primary. We are called to speak the words of God and not our own; to minister the sacraments he has given to his Church; and to call people to a love which he has first made possible.

Hence the surrender to God's call can be made with utmost confidence and without reservation. Our surrender to God's will must be total—the yes given once for all which has as its pattern the yes spoken by Jesus himself. As St. Paul tells us, "As God keeps his word, I declare that my word to you is not yes one minute and no the next. Jesus Christ...was not alternately yes and no; he was never anything but yes" (1 Cor. 1:18-19).

This call of God is grace. It is a gift, a treasure "possessed in earthen vessels to make it clear that its surpassing power comes from God and not from us"

(2 Cor. 4:7). But this gift is not primarily for the priest himself; it is rather a gift of God for the whole Church and for her mission to the world.

Priesthood is an abiding sacramental sign which shows that the love of the Good Shepherd for his flock will never be absent. In my letter to you priests last Holy Thursday, I developed this aspect of the priesthood as God's gift. Our priesthood, I said, "constitutes a special *ministerium,* that is to say service, in relation to the community of believers. It does not, however, take its origin from that community, as though it were the community that 'called' or 'delegated.' The sacramental priesthood is truly a gift for this community and comes from Christ himself, from the fullness of his priesthood" (no. 5). In this gift-giving to his people, it is the divine giver who takes the initiative; it is he who calls the ones "he himself had decided on."

Priesthood Forever and Celibacy

Hence when we reflect on the intimacy between the Lord and his prophet, his priest—an intimacy arising as a result of the call which he has initiated—we can better understand certain characteristics of the priesthood and realize their appropriateness for the Church's mission today as well as in times past:

a) Priesthood is forever—*Tu es sacerdos in aeternum*—we do not return the gift once given. It cannot be that God who gave the impulse to say yes now wishes to hear no.

b) Nor should it surprise the world that the call of God

through the Church continues to offer us a celibate ministry of love and service after the example of our Lord Jesus Christ. God's call has indeed stirred us to the depths of our being. And after centuries of experience, the Church knows how deeply fitting it is that priests should give this concrete response in their lives to express the totality of the yes they have spoken to the Lord who calls them by name to his service.

c) The fact that there is a personal individual call to the priesthood given by the Lord to "the men he himself had decided on" is in accord with the prophetic tradition. It should help us, too, to understand that the Church's traditional decision to call men to the priesthood, and not to call women, is not a statement about human rights, nor an exclusion of women from holiness and mission in the Church. Rather this decision expresses the conviction of the Church about this particular dimension of the gift of priesthood by which God has chosen to shepherd his flock.

The Good Shepherd

3. Dear brothers: "God's flock is in your midst; give it a shepherd's care." How close to the essence of our understanding of priesthood is the role of shepherd. Throughout the history of salvation it is a recurring image of God's care for his people. And only in the role of Jesus, the Good Shepherd, can our pastoral ministry as priests be understood.

Recall how, in the call of the twelve, Jesus summoned them to be his companions precisely in order to "send them out to preach the good news." Priesthood is mission and service; it is being "sent out" from Jesus to "give his flock a shepherd's care." This characteristic of the priest— to apply an excellent phrase about Jesus as the "man for others"—shows us the true sense of what it means to "give a shepherd's care." It means pointing the awareness of humanity to the mystery of God, to the profundity of redemption taking place in Christ Jesus.

Priestly ministry is missionary in its very core. It means being sent out for others, like Christ sent from his Father, for the sake of the Gospel, sent to evangelize. In the words of Paul VI, "evangelizing means bringing the good news into all the strata of humanity...and making it new." (*Evangelii Nuntiandi,* 18).

Fidelity to the magisterium

At the foundation and center of its dynamism, evangelization contains a clear proclamation that salvation is in Jesus Christ, the son of God. It is his name, his teaching, his life, his promises, his kingdom and his mystery that we proclaim to the world. And the effectiveness of our proclamation, and hence the very success of our priesthood, depends on our fidelity to the magisterium, through which the Church guards "the rich deposit of faith with the help of the Holy Spirit who dwells within us" (2 Tm. 1:14).

As a pattern for every ministry and apostolate in the Church, priestly ministry is never to be conceived in terms of an acquisition. Insofar as it is a gift, it is a gift to be proclaimed and shared with others.

Do we not see this clearly in Jesus' teaching when the mother of James and John asked that her sons sit on his right hand and his left in his kingdom? "You know how those who exercise authority among the gentiles lord it over them; their great ones make their importance felt. It cannot be like that with you. Anyone who aspires to greatness must serve the rest, and whoever wants to rank first among you must serve the needs of all. Such is the case with the Son of Man who has come, not to be served by others, but to serve, to give his own life as a ransom for the many" (Mt. 20:25-28).

Just as Jesus was most perfectly a "man for others" in giving himself up totally on the cross, so the priest is most of all servant and "man for others" when he acts in *persona Christi* in the Eucharist, leading the Church in that celebration in which this sacrifice of the cross is renewed. For in the Church's daily Eucharistic worship, the "good news" that the apostles were sent out to proclaim is preached in its fullness; the work of our redemption is reenacted.

How perfectly the fathers at the Second Vatican Council captured this fundamental truth in their Decree on Priestly Life and Ministry:

"The other sacraments, as every ministry of the Church and every work of the apostolate, are linked with the holy Eucharist and are directed toward it...Hence the Eucharist shows itself to be the source and the summit of all evangelization" (*Presbyterorum Ordinis,* 5).

In the celebration of the Eucharist, we priests are at the very heart of our ministry of service, of "giving God's flock a shepherd's care." All our pastoral endeavors are incomplete until our people are led to full and active participation in the Eucharistic sacrifice.

Unity among priests

4. Let us recall how Jesus named twelve as his companions. The call to priestly service includes an invitation to special intimacy with Christ. The lived experience of priests in every generation has led them to discover in their own lives and ministry the absolute centrality of their personal union with Jesus, of being his companions. No one can effectively bring the good news of Jesus to others unless he himself has first been his constant companion through personal prayer, unless he has learned from Jesus the mystery to be proclaimed.

This union with Jesus, modeled on his oneness with his Father, has a further intrinsic dimension, as his own prayer at the Last Supper reveals: "That they may be one, Father, even as we are one" (Jn. 17:11). His priesthood is one and this unity must be actual and effective among his chosen companions. Hence unity among priests, lived out in fraternity and friendship, becomes a demand and an integral part of the life of a priest.

Unity among priests is not a unity or fraternity that is directed toward itself. It is for the sake of the Gospel, to symbolize, in the living out of the priesthood, the essential direction to which the Gospel calls all people: to the union of love with him and one another. And this union alone can guarantee peace and justice and dignity to every human being. Surely this is the underlying sense of the prayer of Jesus when he continues: "I pray also for those who believe in me through their word, that all may be one as you, Father, are in me, and I in you" (Jn. 17:20-21).

Indeed, how will the world come to believe that the Father has sent Jesus unless people can see in visible ways that those who believe in Jesus have heard his commandment to "love one another"? And how will believers receive a witness that such love is a concrete possibility unless they find it in the example of the unity of their priestly ministers, of those whom Jesus himself forms into one priesthood as his own companions?

Zeal to serve

My brother priests: Have we not here touched upon the heart of the matter—our zeal for the priesthood itself? It is inseparable from our zeal for the service of the people.

This concelebrated Mass, which so beautifully symbolizes the unity of our priesthood, gives to the whole world the witness of the unity for which Jesus prayed to his Father on our behalf. But it must not become a merely transient manifestation, which would render fruitless the prayer of Jesus. Every Eucharist renews this prayer for our unity: "Lord, remember your Church throughout the world; make us grow in love, together with John Paul, our Pope...our bishop, and all the clergy."

Your priests' senates, as new structures in the Church, provide a wonderful opportunity to give visible witness to the one priesthood you share with your bishops and with one another, and to demonstrate what must be at the heart of the renewal of every structure in the Church: the unity for which Jesus himself prayed,

5. At the beginning of this homily, I charged you with the task of taking responsibility for your priesthood, a task for each one of you personally, a charge to be shared with all the priests, and especially to be a concern for your priests' councils. The faith of the whole Church needs to have clearly in focus the proper understanding of the priesthood and of its place in the mission of the Church.

So the Church depends on you to deepen ever more this understanding, and to put it into practice in your lives and ministry: in other words, to share the gift of your priesthood with the Church by renewing the response you have already made to Christ's invitation—"Come, follow me" —by giving yourselves as totally as he did.

At times we hear the words, "pray for priests." And today I address these words as an appeal, as a plea, to all the faithful of the Church in the United States. Pray for priests, so that each and every one of them will repeatedly say yes to the call he has received, remain constant in preaching the Gospel message and be faithful forever as the companion of our Lord Jesus Christ.

Dear brother priests: As we renew the paschal mystery and stand as disciples at the foot of the cross with Mary, the mother of Jesus, let us entrust ourselves to her. In her love we shall find strength for our weakness and joy for our hearts.

DES MOINES

Exuberant high school students packing the upper tiers of Madison
Square Garden, New York City, receive the attention and blessing
of Pope John Paul II as he enters the arena.

Wide World Photos

God's Gift—
Man's Responsibility

Homily of the Mass at Living History Farms,
Des Moines, October 4.

Dear brothers and sisters in Christ,

Here in the heartland of America, in the middle of the bountiful fields at harvest time, I come to celebrate the Eucharist. As I stand in your presence in this period of autumn harvest, those words which are repeated whenever people gather for the Eucharist seem to be so appropriate:

"Blessed are you, Lord God of all creation, through your goodness we have this bread to offer which earth has given and human hands have made."

As one who has always been close to nature, let me speak to you today about the land, the earth, and that "which earth has given and human hands have made."

The land is God's gift entrusted to people from the very beginning. It is God's gift, given by a loving Creator as a means of sustaining the life which he had created.

But the land is not only God's gift. It is also man's responsibility. Man, himself created from the dust of the earth (cf. Gn. 3:7), was made its master (cf. Gn. 1:26). In order to bring forth fruit, the land would depend upon the genius and skillfulness, the sweat and the toil of the people to whom God would entrust it.

Thus the food which would sustain life on earth is willed by God to be both that "which earth has given and human hands have made."

To all of you who are farmers and all who are associated with agricultural production, I want to say this: The Church highly esteems your work. Christ himself showed his esteem for agricultural life when he described God his Father as "the Vinedresser" (Jn. 15:1). You cooperate with the Creator, the "Vinedresser," in sustaining and nurturing life. You fulfill the command of God given at the very beginning: "Fill the earth and subdue it" (Gn. 1:28).

Here in the heartland of America, the valleys and hills have been blanketed with grain, the herds and the flocks have multiplied many times over. By hard work you have become masters of the earth and you have subdued it. By reason of the abundant fruitfulness which modern agricultural advances have made possible, you support the lives of millions who themselves do not work on the land, but who live because of what you produce. Mindful of this, I make my own the words of my beloved predecessor Paul VI:

"It is the dignity of those who work on the land and of all those engaged in different levels of research and action in the field of agricultural development which must be unceasingly proclaimed and promoted" (Address to the World Food Conference, November 9, 1974, no. 4).

What then are the attitudes that should pervade man's relationship to the land? As always we must look for the answer beginning with Jesus, for, as St. Paul says: "In your minds you must be the same as Jesus Christ" (Phil. 2:5).

In the life of Jesus, we see a real closeness to the land. In his teaching, he referred to the "birds of the air" (Mt. 6:26), the "lilies of the field" (Mt. 7:17). He talked about the farmer who went out to sow the seed (Mt. 13-4ff). He referred to his heavenly Father as the "Vinedresser" (Jn. 15:1), and to himself as the "Good Shepherd" (Jn. 10:14).

This closeness to nature, this spontaneous awareness of creation as a gift from God, as well as the blessing of a close-knit family—characteristics of farm life in every age including our own—these were part of the life of Jesus. Therefore I invite you to let your attitudes always be the same as those of Christ Jesus.

Gratitude

2. Three attitudes in particular are appropriate for rural life.

In the first place: gratitude. Recall the first words of Jesus in the Gospel we have just heard, words of gratitude to his heavenly Father: "Father, Lord of heaven and earth, to you I offer praise." Let this be your attitude as well. Every day the farmer is reminded of how much depends upon God. From the heavens come the rain, the wind and the sunshine. They occur without the farmer's command or control. The farmer prepares the soil, plants the seed and cultivates the crop. But God makes it grow. He alone is the source of life.

Even the natural disasters, such as hailstorms and drought, tornadoes or floods, remind the farmer of his dependence upon God. Surely it was this awareness that prompted the early pilgrims to America to establish the feast which you call Thanksgiving.

After every harvest, whatever it may have been that year, with humility and thankfulness the farmer makes his own the prayer of Jesus: "Father, Lord of heaven and earth, to you I offer praise."

Second, the land must be conserved with care since it is intended to be fruitful for generation upon generation. You who live in the heartland of America have been entrusted with some of the earth's best land: the soil so rich in minerals, the climate so favorable for producing bountiful crops, with fresh water and unpolluted air available all around you. You are stewards of some of the most important resources God has given to the world. Therefore conserve the land well, so that your children's children and generations after them will inherit an even richer land than was entrusted to you.

But also remember what the heart of your vocation is. While it is true here that farming today provides an economic livelihood for the farmer, still it will always be more than an enterprise of profit-making. In farming, you cooperate with the Creator in the very sustenance of life on earth.

Generosity

In the third place, I want to speak about generosity, a generosity which arises from the fact that "God destined the earth and all it contains for all men and all peoples so that all created things would be shared fairly by all mankind under the guidance of justice tempered by charity" (*Gaudium et Spes,* 69).

You who are farmers today are stewards of a gift from God which was intended for the good of all humanity. You have the potential to provide food for the millions who have nothing to eat and thus help to rid the world of famine. To you I direct the same question asked by Paul VI five years ago:

"If the potential of nature is immense, if that of the mastery of the human genius over the universe seems almost unlimited, what is it that is too often missing... except that generosity, that anxiety which is stimulated by the sight of the sufferings and the miseries of the poor, that deep conviction that the whole family suffers when one of its members is in distress?" (Address to the World Food Conference, November 9, 1974, no. 9).

Recall the time when Jesus saw the hungry crowd gathered on the hillside. What was his response? He did not content himself with expressing his compassion. He gave his disciples the command: "Give them something to eat yourselves" (Mt. 14:16).

Did he not intend those same words for us today, for us who live at the closing of the 20th century, for us who have the means available to feed the hungry of the world? Let us respond generously to his command by sharing the

111

fruit of our labor, by contributing to others the knowledge we have gained, by being the promoters of rural development everywhere and by defending the right to work of the rural population, since every person has a right to useful employment.

Spiritual hunger

3. Farmers everywhere provide bread for all humanity, but it is Christ alone who is the bread of life. He alone satisfies the deepest hunger of humanity. As St. Augustine said: "Our hearts are restless until they rest in you" (Confessions I, 1).

While we are mindful of the physical hunger of millions of our brothers and sisters on all continents, at this Eucharist we are reminded that the deepest hunger lies in the human soul. To all who acknowledge this hunger within them Jesus says: "Come to me, all you who are weary and find life burdensome, and I will refresh you."

My brothers and sisters in Christ: Let us listen to these words with all our heart. They are directed to every one of us. To all who till the soil, to all who benefit from the fruit of their labors, to every man and woman on earth, Jesus says: "Come to me...and I will refresh you." Even if all the physical hunger of the world were satisfied, even if everyone who is hungry were fed by his or her own labor or by the generosity of others, the deepest hunger of man would still exist.

We are reminded in the letter of St. Paul to the Galatians: "All that matters is that one is created anew."

Only Christ can create one anew; and this new creation finds its beginning only in his cross and resurrection. In Christ alone all creation is restored to its proper order. Therefore, I say: Come, all of you, to Christ. He is the bread of life. Come to Christ and you will never be hungry again.

Bring with you to Christ the products of your hands, the fruit of the land, that "which earth has given and human hands have made." At this altar these gifts will be transformed into the Eucharist of the Lord.

Bring with you your efforts to make fruitful the land, your labor and your weariness. At this altar, because of the life, death and resurrection of Christ, all human activity is sanctified, lifted up and fulfilled.

Bring with you the poor, the sick, the exiled and the hungry; bring all who are weary and find life burdensome. At this altar they will be refreshed, for his yoke is easy and his burden light.

Above all, bring your families and dedicate them anew to Christ, so that they may continue to be the working, living and loving community where nature is revered, where burdens are shared and where the Lord is praised in gratitude.

CHICAGO

P. Gnemmi

Your Share
In Christ's Mission

Address to religious brothers in Chicago, October 4.

Brothers in Christ,

1. "I thank my God whenever I think of you; and every time I pray for you, I pray with joy, remembering how you have helped to spread the good news from the day you first heard it right up to the present" (Phil. 1:3-5). These words of St. Paul express my feelings this evening. It is good to be with you. And I am grateful to God for your presence in the Church and for your collaboration in proclaiming the good news.

Brothers, Christ is the purpose and the measure of our lives. In the knowledge of Christ, your vocation took its origin; and in his love, your life is sustained. For he has called you to follow him more closely in a life consecrated through the gift of the evangelical counsels. You follow him in sacrifice and willing generosity. You follow him in joy "singing gratefully to God from your hearts in psalms, hymns and inspired songs" (Col. 3:16). And you follow him in fidelity, even considering it an honor to suffer humiliation for the sake of his name (cf. Acts 5:42).

Your religious consecration is essentially an act of love. It is an imitation of Christ who gave himself to his Father for the salvation of the world. In Christ, the love of his Father and his love for mankind are united. And so it is with you. Your religious consecration has not only deepened your baptismal gift of union with the Trinity, but it has also called you to greater service of the People of God. You are united more closely to the person of Christ, and you share more fully in his mission to the world.

It is about your share in the mission of Christ that I wish to speak this evening.

2. Let me begin by reminding you of the personal qualities needed to share effectively with Christ in his mission. In the first place, you must be interiorly free, spiritually free. The freedom of which I speak is a paradox to many; it is even misunderstood by some who are members of the Church. Nevertheless it is the fundamental human freedom, and it was won for us by Christ on the cross. As St. Paul said, "we were still helpless when at his appointed moment Christ died for sinful men" (Rom. 5:6).

Spiritual freedom

This spiritual freedom, which you received in baptism, you have sought to increase and strengthen through your willing acceptance of the call to follow Jesus more closely in poverty, chastity and obedience. No matter what others may contend or the world may believe, your promises to observe the evangelical counsels have not shackled your freedom: You are not less free because you are obedient; and you are not less loving because of your celibacy. On the contrary, the faithful practice of the evangelical counsels accentuates your human dignity, liberates the human heart and causes your spirit to burn with undivided love for Christ and for his brothers and sisters in the world (cf. *"Perfectae Caritatis,"* 1,12).

But this freedom of an undivided heart (cf. 1 Cor. 7:32-35) must be maintained by continual vigilance and fervent prayer. If you unite yourself continually to Christ in prayer, you shall always be free and ever more eager to share in his mission.

3. Secondly, you must center your life around the Eucharist. While you share in many ways in the passion, death and resurrection of Christ, it is especially in the Eucharist where this is celebrated and made effective. At the Eucharist, your spirit is renewed, your mind and heart are refreshed and you will find the strength to live day by day for him who is the Redeemer of the world.

4. Thirdly, be dedicated to God's word. Remember the words of Jesus: "My mother and my brothers are those who hear the word of God and put it into practice" (Lk. 8:21). If you sincerely listen to God's word, and humbly but persistently try to put it into practice, like the seed sown in fertile soil, his word will bear fruit in your life.

5. The fourth and final element which makes effective your sharing in Christ's mission is fraternal life. Your life lived in religious community is the first concrete expression of love of neighbor. It is there that the first

demands of self-sacrifice and generous service are exercised in order to build up the fraternal community. This love which unites you as brothers in community becomes in turn the force which supports you in your mission for the Church.

A splendid heritage

6. Brothers in Christ, today the universal Church honors St. Francis of Assisi. As I think of this great saint, I am reminded of his delight in God's creation, his childlike simplicity, his poetic marriage to "Lady Poverty," his missionary zeal and his desire to share fully in the cross of Christ. What a splendid heritage he has handed on to those among you who are Franciscans, and to all of us.

Similarly, God has raised up many other men and women outstanding in holiness. These too he destined to found religious families which, each in a distinctive way, would play an important role in the mission of the Church. The key to the effectiveness of every one of these religious institutes has been their faithfulness to the original charism God has begun in their founder or foundress for the enrichment of the Church. For this reason, I repeat the words of Paul VI: "Be faithful to the spirit of your founders, to their evangelical intentions and to the example of their holiness... It is precisely here that the dynamism proper to each religious family finds its origin" ("Evangelica Testificatio," 11-12). And this remains a secure basis for judging what specific ecclesial activities each institute, and every individual member, should undertake in order to fulfill the mission of Christ.

7. Never forget the specific and ultimate aim of all apostolic service: to lead the men and women of our day to communion with the most Holy Trinity. In the present age, mankind is increasingly tempted to seek security in possessions, knowledge and power. By the witness of your life consecrated to Christ in poverty, chastity and obedience, you challenge this false security. You are a living reminder that Christ alone is "the Way, the Truth and the Life" (Jn. 14:6).

8. Religious brothers today are involved in a wide range of activities: teaching in Catholic schools, spreading God's word in missionary activity, responding to a variety of human needs by both your witness and your actions, and serving by prayer and sacrifice. As you go forward in your particular service, keep in mind the advice of St. Paul: "Whatever you do, work at it with your whole being. Do it for the Lord rather than for men" (Col. 3:23). For the measure of your effectiveness will be the degree of your love for Jesus Christ.

9. Finally, every form of apostolic service, of either an individual or a community, must be in accord with the Gospel as it is put forward by the magisterium. For all Christian service incorporates Gospel values. Therefore be men of God's word: men whose hearts burn within them when they hear the word proclaimed (cf. Lk. 24:32); who shape every action according to its demands; and who desire to see the Good News proclaimed to the ends of the earth.

Brothers, your presence in the Church and your collaboration in promoting the Gospel are an encouragement and joy to me in my role as pastor of the whole Church. May God give each of you long life. May he call many others to follow Christ in the religious life. And may the Virgin Mary, Mother of the Church and model of consecrated life, obtain for you the joy and consolation of Christ her Son.

A Ministry of
Holiness and Truth

Address to the American bishops, Chicago, October 5.

Dear Brothers in Our Lord Jesus Christ,

1. May I tell you very simply how grateful I am to you for your invitation to come to the United States. It is an immense joy for me to make this pastoral visit, and in particular, to be here with you today.

On this occasion I thank you, not only for your invitation, not only for everything you have done to prepare for my visit, but also for your partnership in the Gospel from the time of my election as Pope.

I thank you for your service to God's holy people, for your fidelity to Christ our Lord and for your unity with my predecessors and with me in the Church and in the college of bishops.

I wish at this time to render public homage to a long tradition of fidelity to the Apostolic See on the part of the American hierarchy. During the course of two centuries, this tradition has edified your people, authenticated your apostolate and enriched the universal Church.

Moreover, in your presence today I wish to acknowledge with deep appreciation the fidelity of your faithful and the renowned vitality that they have shown in

Christian life. This vitality has been manifested not only in the sacramental practice of communities but also in abundant fruits of the Holy Spirit.

With great zeal your people have endeavored to build up the kingdom of God by means of the Catholic school and through all catechetical efforts. An evident concern for others has been a real part of American Catholicism, and today I thank the American Catholics for their generosity. Their support has benefited the dioceses of the United States and a widespread network of charitable works and self-help projects, including those sponsored by Catholic Relief Services and the Campaign for Human Development.

Moreover, the help given to the missions by the Church in the United States remains a lasting contribution to the cause of Christ's Gospel. Because your faithful have been very generous to the Apostolic See, my predecessors have been assisted in meeting the burdens of their office; and thus, in the exercise of their worldwide mission of charity, they have been able to extend help to those in need, thereby showing the concern of the universal Church for all humanity. For me, then, this is an hour of solemn gratitude.

Pastor of the whole Church

2. But even more, this is an hour of ecclesial communion and fraternal love. I come to you as a brother bishop: one who, like yourselves, has known the hopes and challenges of a local church, one who has worked within the structures of a diocese, who has collaborated within

the framework of an episcopal conference; one who has known the exhilarating experience of collegiality in an ecumenical council as exercised by bishops together with him who both presided over this collegial assembly and was recognized by it as *totius ecclesiae pastor*—invested with "full, supreme and universal power over the Church" (cf. *Lumen Gentium,* 22).

I come to you as one who has been personally edified and enriched by participation in the Synod of Bishops; one who was supported and assisted by the fraternal interest and self-giving of American bishops who traveled to Poland in order to express solidarity with the Church in my country.

I come as one who found deep spiritual consolation for my pastoral activity in the encouragement of the Roman Pontiff with whom, and under whom, I served God's people, and in particular in the encouragement of Paul VI, whom I looked upon not only as head of the college of bishops, but also as my own spiritual father.

And today, under the sign of collegiality and because of a mysterious design of God's providence, I, your brother in Jesus, now come to you as successor of Peter in the See of Rome, and therefore as pastor of the whole Church.

Because of my personal pastoral responsibility, and because of our common pastoral responsibility for the people of God in the United States, I desire to strengthen you in your ministry of faith as local pastors, and to support you in your individual and joint pastoral activities by encouraging you to stand fast in the holiness and truth of our Lord Jesus Christ. And in you I desire to honor Jesus Christ, the Shepherd and Bishop of our souls (cf 1 Pt. 2:25).

Because we have been called to be shepherds of the flock, we realize that we must present ourselves as humble servants of the Gospel. Our leadership will be effective only to the extent that our own discipleship is genuine—to the extent that the Beatitudes have become the inspiration of our lives, to the extent that our people really find in us the kindness, simplicity of life and universal charity that they expect.

We who, by divine mandate, must proclaim the duties of the Christian law, and who must call our people to constant conversion and renewal, know that St. Paul's invitation applies above all to ourselves: "You must put on the new man created in God's image, whose justice and holiness are born of truth" (Eph. 4:24).

Holiness: priority of our ministry

3. The holiness of personal conversion is indeed the condition for our fruitful ministry as bishops of the Church. It is our union with Jesus Christ that determines the credibility of our witness to the Gospel and the supernatural effectiveness of our activity. We can convincingly proclaim "the unsearchable riches of Christ" (Eph. 3:8) only if we maintain fidelity to the love and friendship of Jesus, only if we continue to live in the faith of the Son of God.

God has given a great gift to the American hierarchy in recent years: the canonization of John Neumann. An American bishop is officially held up by the Catholic

Church to be an exemplary servant of the Gospel and shepherd of God's people, above all because of his great love of Christ.

On the occasion of the canonization, Paul VI asked: "What is the meaning of this extraordinary event, the meaning of this canonization?" And he answered, saying: "It is the celebration of holiness." And this holiness of St. John Neumann was expressed in brotherly love, in pastoral charity and in zealous service by one who was the bishop of a diocese and an authentic disciple of Christ.

During the canonization, Paul VI went on to say: "Our ceremony today is indeed the celebration of holiness. At the same time, it is a prophetic anticipation—for the church, for the United States, for the world—of a renewal of love: love for God, love for neighbor." As bishops, we are called to exercise in the church this prophetic role of love and, therefore, of holiness.

Guided by the Holy Spirit, we must all be deeply convinced that holiness is the first priority in our lives and in our ministry. In this context, as bishops we see the immense value of prayer: the liturgical prayer of the church, our prayer together, our prayer alone.

In recent times many of you have found that the practice of making spiritual retreats together with your brother bishops is indeed a help to that holiness born of truth. May God sustain you in this initiative: so that each of you, and all of you together, may fulfill your role as a sign of holiness offered to God's people on their pilgrimage to the Father.

May you yourselves, like St. John Neumann, also be a

prophetic anticipation of holiness. The people need to have bishops who are trying to anticipate prophetically in their own lives the attainment of the goal to which they are leading the faithful.

Consecrated in truth

4. St. Paul points out the relationship of justice and holiness to truth (cf. Eph. 4:24). Jesus himself, in his priestly prayer, asks his Father to consecrate his disciples by means of truth. And he adds: "Your word is truth"—*sermo tuus veritas est* (Jn. 17:17). And he goes on to say that he consecrates himself for the sake of the disciples, so that they themselves may be consecrated in truth.

Jesus consecrated himself so that the disciples might be consecrated, set apart, by the communication of what he was: the truth. Jesus tells his Father: "I gave them your word"—"Your word is truth" (Jn. 17:14,17).

The holy word of God, which is truth, is commmunicated by Jesus to his disciples. This word is entrusted as a sacred deposit to his Church, but only after he had implanted in his Church, through the power of the Holy Spirit, a special charism to guard and transmit intact the word of God.

With great wisdom, John XXIII convoked the Second Vatican Council. Reading the signs of the times, he knew that what was needed was a council of a pastoral nature, a council that would reflect the great pastoral love and care of Jesus Christ the Good Shepherd for his people. But he knew that a pastoral council—to be genuinely effective—would need a strong doctrinal basis. And precisely for this reason, precisely because the word of God is the only basis for every pastoral initiative, John XXIII on the opening day of the Council—October 11, 1962—made the following statement: "The greatest concern of the Ecumenical Council is this: that the sacred deposit of Christian doctrine should be more effectively guarded and taught."

To guard and teach doctrine

This explains Pope John's inspiration. This is what the new Pentecost was to be. This is why the bishops of the Church—in the greatest manifestation of collegiality in the history of the world—were called together: "so that the sacred deposit of Christian doctrine should be more effectively guarded and taught."

In our time, Jesus was consecrating anew his disciples by truth, and he was doing it by means of an ecumenical council. He was transmitting by the power of the Holy Spirit his Father's word to new generations. And, what John XXIII considered to be the aim of the Council, I consider as the aim of this postconciliar period.

For this reason, in my first meeting last November with American bishops on their *ad limina* visit I stated: "This then is my own deepest hope today for the pastors of the church in America, as well as for all the pastors of the universal Church: that the sacred deposit of Christian doctrine should be more effectively guarded and taught."

In the word of God is the salvation of the world. By means of the proclamation of the word of God, the Lord continues in his Church and through his Church to consecrate his disciples, communicating to them the truth that he himself is.

For this reason the Vatican Council emphasized the bishop's role of announcing the full truth of the Gospel and proclaiming "the whole mystery of Christ" (*Christus Dominus,* 12). This teaching was constantly repeated by Paul VI for the edification of the universal Church. It was explicity proclaimed by John Paul I on the very day he died and I too have frequently reaffirmed it in my own pontificate. And I am sure that my successors and your successors will hold this teaching until Christ comes again in glory.

Letter from a Bishop

5. Among the papers that were left to me by Paul VI there is a letter written to him by a bishop on the occasion of the latter's appointment to the episcopacy.

It is a beautiful letter; and in the form of a resolution it includes a clear affirmation of the bishop's role of guarding and teaching the deposit of Christian doctrine, of proclaiming the whole mystery of Christ. Because of the splendid insights that this letter offers, I would like to share part of it with you.

As he pledged himself to be loyal in obedience to Paul VI and to his successors, the bishop wrote: "I am resolved:

—"To be faithful and constant in proclaiming the Gospel of Christ.

—"To maintain the content of faith, entire and uncorrupted, as handed down by the apostles and professed by the Church at all times and places."

And then with equal insight, this bishop went on to tell Paul VI that, with the help of almighty God, he was determined:

—"To build up the Church as the body of Christ, and to remain united to it by your link, with the order of bishops, under the authority of the successor of St. Peter the apostle.

—"To show kindness and compassion in the name of the Lord to the poor and to strangers and to all who are in need.

—"To seek out the sheep who stray and to gather them into the fold of the Lord.

—"To pray without ceasing for the people of God, to carry out the highest duties of the priesthood in such a way as to afford no grounds for reproof."

This then is the edifying witness of a bishop, an American bishop, to the episcopal ministry of holiness and truth. These words are a credit to him and a credit to all of you.

A challenge for our age

A challenge for our age—and for every age in the Church—is to bring the message of the Gospel to the very core of our people's lives—so that they may live the full truth of their humanity, their redemption and their adoption in Jesus Christ—that they may be enriched with "the justice and holiness of truth."

6. In the exercise of your ministry of truth, as bishops of the United States you have, through statements and pastoral letters, collectively offered the word of God to your people, showing its relevance to daily life, pointing to the power it has to uplift and heal, and at the same time upholding its inherent demands. Three years ago you did this in a very special way through your pastoral letter, so beautifully titled "To Live in Christ Jesus." This letter, in which you offered your people the service of truth, contains a number of points to which I wish to allude today.

With compassion, understanding and love, you transmitted a message that is linked to revelation and to the mystery of faith. And so with great pastoral charity you spoke of God's love, of humanity and of sin—and of the meaning of redemption and of life in Christ.

You spoke of the word of Christ as it affects individuals, the family, the community and nations. You spoke of justice and peace, of charity, of truth and friendship. And you spoke of some special questions affecting the moral life of Christians: the moral life in its individual and social aspects.

You spoke explicitly of the Church's duty to be faithful to the mission entrusted to her. And precisely for this reason you spoke of certain issues that needed a clear reaffirmation, because Catholic teaching in their regard had been challenged, denied or in practice violated.

You repeatedly proclaimed human rights and human dignity and the incomparable worth of people of every racial and ethnic origin, declaring that "racial antagonism and discrimination are among the most persistent and destructive evils of our nation." You forcefully rejected the oppression of the weak, the manipulation of the vulnerable, the waste of goods and resources, the ceaseless preparations for war, unjust social structures and policies and all crimes by and against individuals and against creation.

Doctrine on marriage

With the candor of the Gospels, the compassion of pastors and the charity of Christ, you faced the question of the indissolubility of marriage, rightly stating: "The covenant between a man and a woman joined in Christian marriage is as indissoluble and irrevocable as God's love for his people and Christ's love for his Church."

In exalting the beauty of marriage you rightly spoke against both the ideology of contraception and contraceptive acts, as did the encyclical *Humanae Vitae.* And I myself today, with the same conviction of Paul VI, ratify the teaching of this encyclical, which was put forth by my predecessor "by virtue of the mandate entrusted to us by Christ" (*AAS,*60, 1968, p. 485).

In portraying the sexual union between husband and wife as a special expression of their covenanted love, you rightly stated: "Sexual intercourse is a moral and human good only within marriage, outside marriage it is wrong."

As "men with the message of truth and the power of good" (2 Cor. 6:7), as authentic teachers of God's law and as compassionate pastors you also rightly stated: "Homosexual activity...as distinguished from homosexual orientation, is morally wrong." In the clarity of this truth, you exemplified the real charity of Christ; you did not betray those people who, because of homosexuality, are confronted with difficult moral problems, as would have happened if, in the name of understanding and compassion, or for any other reason, you had held out false hope to any brother or sister. Rather, by your witness to the truth of humanity in God's plan, you effectively manifested fraternal love, upholding the true dignity, the true human dignity, of those who look to Christ's Church for the guidance which comes from the light of God's word.

You also gave witness to the truth, thereby serving all humanity, when, echoing the teaching of the Council— "from the moment of conception life must be guarded with the greatest care" (*Gaudium et Spes,* 51),—you reaffirmed the right to life and the inviolability of every human life, including the life of unborn children. You clearly said: "To destroy these innocent unborn children is an unspeakable crime... Their right to life must be recognized and fully protected by the law."

And just as you defended the unborn in the truth of their being, so also you clearly spoke up for the aged, asserting: "Euthanasia or mercy killing... is a grave moral evil... Such killing is incompatible with respect for human dignity and reverence for life."

And in your pastoral interest for your people in all their needs—including housing, education, health care, employment and the administration of justice—you gave further witness to the fact that all aspects of human life are sacred. You were, in effect, proclaiming that the

Church will never abandon man, nor his temporal needs, as she leads humanity to salvation and eternal life.

And because the Church's greatest act of fidelity to humanity and the "fundamental function in every age and particularly in ours is to direct man's gaze, to point the awareness and experience of the whole of humanity toward the mystery of God's (*Redemptor Hominis,* 10)— because of this you rightly alluded to the dimension of eternal life. It is indeed in this proclamation of eternal life that we hold up a great motive of hope for our people. Against the onslaughts of materialism, against rampant secularism and against moral permissiveness.

Responsible pastoral initiatives

7. A sense of pastoral responsibility has also been genuinely expressed by individual bishops in their ministry as local pastors. To the great credit of their authors I would cite but two recent examples of pastoral letters issued in the United States. Both are examples of responsible pastoral initiatives. One of them deals with the issue of racism and vigorously denounces it. The other refers to homosexuality and deals with the issue, as should be done, with clarity and great pastoral charity, thus rendering a real service to truth and to those who are seeking this liberating truth.

Brothers in Christ: As we proclaim the truth in love, it is not possible for us to avoid all criticism; nor is it possible to please everyone. But it is possible to work for the real benefit of everyone. And so we are humbly convinced that God is with us in our ministry of truth, and that he "did not give us a spirit of timidity but a spirit of power and love and self-control" (2 Tm. 1:7).

One of the greatest rights of the faithful is to receive the word of God in its purity and integrity as guaranteed by the magisterium of the universal church: the authentic magisterium of the bishops of the Catholic Church teaching in union with the Pope.

Dear brothers: we can be assured that the Holy Spirit is assisting us in our teaching if we remain absolutely faithful to the universal magisterium.

Charism and magisterium

In this regard I wish to add an extremely important point which I recently emphasized in speaking to a group of bishops making their ad *limina* visit:

"In the community of the faithful—which must always maintain Catholic unity with the bishops and the Apostolic See—there are great insights of faith. The Holy Spirit is active in enlightening the minds of the faithful with his truth and in inflaming their hearts with his love. But these insights of faith and this *sensus fidelium* are not independent of the magisterium of the Church, which is an instrument of the same Holy Spirit and is assisted by him.

"It is only when the faithful have been nourished by the word of God, faithfully transmitted in its purity and integrity, that their own charisms are fully operative and fruitful. Once the word of God is faithfully proclaimed to the community and is accepted, it brings forth fruits of justice and holiness of life in abundance.

"But the dynamism of the community in understanding and living the word of God depends on its receiving intact the *depositum fidei;* and for this precise purpose a special apostolic and pastoral charism has been given to the Church. It is one and the same spirit of truth who directs the hearts of the faithful and who guarantees the magisterium of the pastors of the flock."

Christian Unity

8. One of the greatest truths of which we are the humble custodians is the doctrine of the Church's unity—that unity which is tarnished on the human face of the Church by every form of sin, but which subsists indestructibly in the Catholic Church (cf. *Lumen Gentium,* 8; *Unitatis Redintegratio,* 2, 3). A consciousness of sin calls us incessantly to conversion. The will of Christ impels us to work earnestly and perseveringly for unity with all our Christian brethren, being mindful that the unity we seek is one of perfect faith, a unity in truth and love.

We must pray and study together, knowing however, that intercommunion between divided Christians is not the answer to Christ's appeal for perfect unity. And with God's help we will continue to work humbly and resolutely to remove the real divisions that still exist, and thus to restore that full unity in faith which is the condition for sharing in the Eucharist (cf. Address of May 4, 1979).

The commitment of the Ecumenical Council belongs to each of us, as does the testament of Paul VI, who, writing on ecumenism, stated: "Let the work of drawing near to our separated brethren go on, with much understanding, with much patience, with great love; but without deviating from the true Catholic doctrine."

9. As bishops who are servants of truth, we are also called to be servants of unity, in the communion of the Church.

A call to conversion

In the communion of holiness we ourselves are called, as I mentioned above, to conversion, so that we may preach with convincing power the message of Jesus: "Reform your lives and believe in the Gospel."

We have a special role to play in safeguarding the sacrament of reconciliation, so that in fidelity to a divine precept, we and our people may experience in our innermost being that "grace has far surpassed sin" (Rom. 5:20). I, too, ratify the prophetic call of Paul VI, who urged the bishops to help their priests to "deeply understand how closely they collaborate through the sacrament of penance with the Savior in the work of conversion" (Address of April 20, 1978).

In this regard I confirm again the norms of *Sacramentum Paenitentiae* which so wisely emphasize the ecclesial dimension of the sacrament of penance and indicate the precise limits of general absolution, just as Paul VI did in his *ad limina* address to the American bishops.

Conversion by its very nature is the condition for that union with God which reaches its greatest expression in the Eucharist. Our union with Christ in the Eucharist presupposes, in turn, that our hearts are set on conversion, that they are pure. This is indeed an important part of our preaching to the people.

In my encyclical I endeavored to express it in these words: "The Christ who calls to the Eucharistic banquet is always the same Christ who exhorts us to penance and repeats his 'repent.' Without this constant and ever-renewed endeavor for conversion, partaking of the Eucharist would lack its full redeeming effectiveness..." (*Redemptor Hominis*, 20).

Need for confession

In the face of a widespread phenomenon of our time, namely that many of our people who are among the great numbers who receive Communion make little use of confession, we must emphasize Christ's basic call to conversion. We must also stress that the personal encounter with the forgiving Jesus in the sacrament of reconciliation is a divine means which keeps alive in our hearts and in our communities a consciousness of sin in its perennial and tragic reality, and which actually brings forth, by the action of Jesus and the power of his spirit, fruits of conversion in justice and holiness of life. By this sacrament we are renewed in fervor, strengthened in our resolves and buoyed by divine encouragement.

10. As chosen leaders in a community of praise and prayer, it is our special joy to offer the Eucharist and to give our people a sense of their vocation as an Easter people, with the "alleluia" as their song. And let us always recall that the validity of all liturgical development and the effectiveness of every liturgical sign pre-

supposes the great principle that the Catholic liturgy is theocentric, and that it is above all "the worship of divine majesty" (cf. *Sacrosanctum Concilium,* 33), in union with Jesus Christ.

Our people have a supernatural sense whereby they look for reverence in all liturgy, especially in what touches the mystery of the Eucharist. With deep faith our people understand that the Eucharist—in the Mass and outside the Mass—is the body and blood of Jesus Christ, and therefore deserves the worship that is given to the living God and to him alone.

As ministers of a community of service, it is our privilege to proclaim the truth of Christ's union with his members in his body, the Church. Hence we commend all service rendered in his name and to his brethren (cf. Mt. 25:45).

In a community of witness and evangelization may our testimony be clear and without reproach. In this regard the Catholic press and the other means of social communication are called to fulfill a special role of great dignity at the service of truth and charity. The Church's aim in employing and sponsoring these media is linked to her mission of evangelization and of service to humanity; through the media the Church hopes to promote ever more effectively the uplifting message of the Gospel.

Unity through fidelity

11. And each individual church over which you preside and which you serve is a community founded on the word of God and acting in the truth of this word. It is in

fidelity to the communion of the universal Church that our local unity is authenticated and made stable.

In the communion of the universal Church local churches find their own identity and enrichment ever more clearly. But all of this requires that the individual churches should maintain complete openness toward the universal Church.

And this is the mystery that we celebrate today in proclaiming the holiness and truth and unity of the episcopal ministry.

Brothers: This ministry of ours makes us accountable to Christ and to his Church. Jesus Christ, the Chief Shepherd (1 Pt. 5:4), loves us and sustains us. It is he who transmits his Father's word and consecrates us in truth, so that each of us may say in turn of our people: "For them I consecrate myself for their sake now, that they may be consecrated in truth." (Jn. 17:19).

Let us pray for and devote special energy to promoting and maintaining vocations to the sacred priesthood, so that the pastoral care of the priestly ministry may be ensured for future generations. I ask you to call upon parents and families, upon priests, religious and laity to unite in fulfilling this vital responsibility of the entire community. And to the young people themselves let us hold up the full challenge of following Christ and of embracing his invitation with full generosity.

As we ourselves pursue every day the justice and holiness born of truth, let us look to Mary, mother of Jesus, Queen of Apostles and cause of our joy.

May St. Frances Xavier Cabrini, St. Elizabeth Ann

Seton and St. John Neumann pray for you, and for all the people whom you are called to serve in holiness and truth and in the unity of Christ and his Church.

Dear brothers: "Grace be with all who love our Lord Jesus Christ with unfailing love" (Eph. 5:24).

F. Dolan

Words of affection and loyalty in Polish—with English translation below—are displayed on a banner hung from a street pole by the residence of the Vatican Observer to the UN.

The Church's Unity in Love

Homily of the Mass in Grant Park, Chicago, October 5.

My brothers and sisters in Jesus Christ,

The readings of today's celebration place us immediately before the deep mystery of our calling as Christians.

Before Jesus was taken up to heaven, he gathered his disciples around him, and he explained to them once more the meaning of his mission of salvation: "Thus it is written," he said, "that the Messiah must suffer and rise from the dead on the third day. In his name, penance for the remission of sins is to be preached to all nations" (Lk. 24:46-47). At the moment that he took leave of his apostles he commanded them, and through them the whole Church, each one of us: to go out and bring the message of redemption to all nations. St. Paul expresses this forcefully in his second letter to the Corinthians: "He has entrusted the message of reconciliation to us. This makes us ambassadors of Christ. God as it were appealing through us" (2 Cor. 5:19-20).

Once again, the Lord places us fully in the mystery of humanity, a humanity that is in need of salvation. And

God has willed that the salvation of humanity should take place through the humanity of Christ, who for our sake died and was raised up (cf. 2 Cor. 5:15), and who also entrusted his redeeming mission to us. Yes, we are truly "ambassadors for Christ," and workers for evangelization.

In the apostolic exhortation *"Evangelii Nuntiandi,"* which he wrote at the request of the third general assembly of the Synod of Bishops, my predecessor in the See of St. Peter, Paul VI, invited the whole People of God to meditate on their basic duty of evangelization. He invited each one of us to examine in what way we might be true witnesses to the message of redemption, in what way we might communicate to others the good news that we have received from Jesus through his Church.

A test of credibility

There are certain conditions that are necessary if we are to share in the evangelizing mission of the Church. This afternoon, I wish to stress one of these conditions in particular. I am speaking about the unity of the Church, our unity in Jesus Christ. Let me repeat what Paul VI said about this unity: "The Lord's spiritual testament tells us that unity among his followers is not only the proof that we are his, but also the proof that he is sent by the Father. It is the test of credibility of Christians and of Christ himself... Yes, the destiny of evangelization is certainly bound up with the witness of unity given by the Church" (*"Evangelii Nuntiandi,"* 77).

I am prompted to choose this particular aspect of

evangelization by looking at the thousands of people whom I see gathered around me today. When I lift up my eyes, I see in you the People of God, united to sing the praises of the Lord and to celebrate his Eucharist. I see also the whole people of America, one nation formed of many people: *E pluribus unum.*

In the first two centuries of your history as a nation, you have travelled a long road, always in search of a better future, in search of stable employment, in search of a homestead. You have travelled "From sea to shining sea" to find your identity, to discover each other along the way, and to find your own place in this immense country.

Your ancestors came from many different countries across the oceans to meet here with the people of different communities that were already established here. In every generation, the process has been repeated: new groups arrive, each one with a different history, to settle here and become part of something new. The same process still goes on when families move from the south to the north, from the east to the west. Each time they come with their own past to a new town or a new city, to become part of a new community. The pattern repeats itself over and over: *E pluribus unum*—the many form a new unity.

Yes, something new was created every time. You brought with you a different culture and you contributed your own distinctive richness to the whole; you had different skills and you put them to work, complementing each other, to create industry, agriculture and business; each group carried with it different human values and shared them with the others for the enrichment of your nation. *E pluribus unum:* you became a new entity, a new people, the true nature of which cannot be adequately explained as a mere putting together of various communities.

Growing in understanding

And so, looking at you, I see people who have thrown their destinies together and now write a common history. Different as you are, you have come to accept each other, at times imperfectly and even to the point of subjecting each other to various forms of discrimination; at times only after a long period of misunderstanding and rejection; even now still growing in understanding and appreciation of each other's differences.

In expressing gratitude for the many blessings you have received, you also become aware of the duty you have toward the less favored in your own midst and in the rest of the world—a duty of sharing, of loving, of serving. As a people, you recognize God as the source of your many blessings, and you are open to his love and his law.

This is America in her ideal and her resolution: "one nation, under God, indivisible, with liberty and justice for all." This is the way America was conceived. This is what she was called to be. And for all this, we offer thanks to the Lord.

But there is another reality that I see when I look at you. It is even deeper, and more demanding than the common history and union which you built from the richness of your different cultural and ethnic heritages— those heritages that you now rightly want to know and to preserve. History does not exhaust itself in material progress, in technological conquest, or in cultural achievement only. Coming together around the altar of sacrifice to break the bread of the holy Eucharist with the successor of Peter, you testify to this even deeper reality: to your unity as members of the people of God.

"We, though many, are one body in Christ" (Rom. 12:5). The Church too is composed of many members and enriched by the diversity of those who make up the one community of faith and baptism, the one Body of Christ. What brings us together and makes us one is our faith—the one apostolic faith.

We are all one, because we have accepted Jesus Christ as the Son of God, the redeemer of the human race, the sole mediator between God and man. By the sacrament of baptism we have been truly incorporated into the crucified and glorified Christ, and through the action of the Holy Spirit we have become living members of his one Body. Christ gave us the wonderful sacrament of the Eucharist by which the unity of the Church is both expressed and continually brought about and perfected.

One Lord, one faith, one baptism

"One Lord, one faith, one baptism" (Eph. 4:5), thus we are all bound together, as the people of God, the Body of Christ, in a unity that transcends the diversity of our origin, culture, education and personality—in a unity that does not exclude a rich diversity in ministries and services. With St. Paul we proclaim: "Just as each of us has one body with many members, and not all the members have the same function, so too we, though many, are one Body in Christ, and individually members one of another'' (Rom. 12:4-5).

If then the Church, the one Body of Christ, is to be a forcefully discernible sign of the gospel message, all her members must show forth, in the words of Paul VI, that ''harmony and consistency of doctrine, life and worship which marked the first days of her existence'' (Apostolic Exhortation on Reconciliation within the Church, 2), when Christians ''devoted themselves to the apostles' teachings and fellowship, to the breaking of bread and the prayers'' (Acts 2:42).

Our unity in faith must be complete, lest we fail to witness to the Gospel, lest we cease to be evangelizing. No local ecclesial community therefore can cut itself off from the treasure of the faith as proclaimed by the Church's teaching office, for it is to this teaching office of the Church, to this magisterium, that the deposit of faith has been especially entrusted by Christ.

With Paul VI I attest to the great truth: ''While being translated into all expressions, the content of the faith must be neither impaired nor mutilated. While being clothed with the outward forms proper to each people...it must remain the content of the Catholic faith just exactly as the ecclesial magisterium has received it and transmits it'' (*Evangelii Nuntiandi, 65*).

Finally, and above all, the mission of evangelization that is mine and yours, must be carried out through a constant, unselfish witnessing to the unity of love. Love is the force that opens hearts to the word of Jesus and to his redemption. Love is the only basis for human relationships that respect in one another the dignity of the children of God, created in his image and saved by the death and resurrection of Jesus. Love is the only driving force that impels us to share with our brothers and sisters all that we are and have.

Love is the power that gives rise to dialogue, in which we listen to each other and learn from each other. Love gives rise, above all, to the dialogue of prayer in which we listen to God's word, which is alive in the Holy Bible and alive in the life of the Church.

Love builds bridges

Let love then build the bridges across our differences and at times our contrasting positions. Let love for each other and love for the truth be the answer to polarization, when factions are formed because of differing views in matters that relate to faith or to the priorities for action.

No one in the ecclesial community should ever feel alienated or unloved, even when tensions arise in the course of the common efforts to bring the fruits of the Gospel to society around us. Our unity as Christians, as Catholics, must always be a unity of love in Jesus Christ our Lord.

In a few moments, we shall celebrate our unity by renewing the sacrifice of Christ. Each one will bring a different gift to be presented in union with the offering of Jesus: dedication to the betterment of society; efforts to console those who suffer; the desire to give witness for justice; the resolve to work for peace and brotherhood; the joy of a united family; or suffering in body or mind.

Different gifts, yes, but all united in the one great gift of Christ's love for his Father and for us—everything united in the unity of Christ and his sacrifice.

And in the strength and power, in the joy and peace of this sacred unity, we pledge ourselves anew—as one people—to fulfill the command of our Lord Jesus Christ: Go and teach all people my Gospel. By word and example give witness to my name. And behold, I am with you always, until the end of the world.

WASHINGTON

Mary: the Woman
of Faith

Remarks to priests at St. Matthew's Cathedral,
Washington, October 6.

Mary says to us today: "I am the servant of the Lord. Let it be done to me as you say" (Lk. 1:38).

And with those words, she expresses what was the fundamental attitude of her life: her faith! Mary believed! She trusted in God's promises and was faithful to his will. When the angel Gabriel announced that she was chosen to be the mother of the Most High, she gave her "Fiat" humbly and with full freedom: "Let it be done to me as you say."

Perhaps the best description of Mary and, at the same time, the greatest tribute to her, was the greeting of her cousin Elizabeth; "Blessed is she who trusted that God's words to her would be fulfilled" (Luke 1:45). For it was that continual trust in the providence of God which most characterized her faith.

All her earthly life was a "pilgrimage of faith" (cf. *"Lumen Gentium,"* 58). For like us she walked in shadows and hoped for things unseen. She knew the

155

contradictions of our earthly life. She was promised that her Son would be given David's throne, but at his birth, there was no room even at the inn. Mary still believed. The angel said her child would be called the Son of God; but she would see him slandered, betrayed and condemned, and left to die as a thief on the cross. Even yet, Mary "trusted that God's words to her would be fulfilled" (Luke 1:45) and that "nothing was impossible with God" (Luke 1:37).

This woman of faith, Mary of Nazareth, the Mother of God, has been given to us as a model in our pilgrimage of faith. From Mary we learn to surrender to God's will in all things. From Mary, we learn to trust even when all hope seems gone. From Mary, we learn to love Christ, her Son and the Son of God. For Mary is not only the Mother of God, she is Mother of the Church as well. In every stage of the march through history, the Church has benefited from the prayer and protection of the Virgin Mary. Holy Scripture and the experience of the faithful see the Mother of God as the one who in a very special way is united with the Church at the most difficult moments in her history, when attacks on the Church become most threatening. Precisely in periods when Christ, and therefore his Church, provokes premeditated contradiction, Mary appears particularly close to the Church, because for her the Church is always her beloved Christ.

I therefore exhort you in Christ Jesus, to continue to look to Mary as the model of the Church, as the best example of the discipleship of Christ. Learn from her to be always faithful, to trust that God's word to you will be fulfilled, and that nothing is impossible with God. Turn to Mary frequently in your prayer "for never was it known that anyone who fled to her protection, implored her help or sought her intercession was left unaided."

As a great sign that has appeared in the heavens, Mary guides and sustains us on our pilgrim way, urging us on to "the victory that overcomes the world, our faith" (1 John 5:5).

In Washington, D.C., the Holy Father reemphasized the need for Americans to hold to values that are older and deeper than consumerism, and he challenged some of the basic structures of the modern world.

C. Slattery

Human Values and
The Common Good

Speech on the White House south lawn, October 6.

Mr. President. I am honored to have had, at your kind invitation, the opportunity for a meeting with you; for by your office as President of the United States of America you represent before the world the whole American nation and you hold the immense responsibility of leading this nation in the path of justice and peace.

I thank you publicly for this meeting and I thank all those who have contributed to its success. I wish also to reiterate here my deep gratitude for the warm welcome and the many kindnesses which I have received from the American people on my pastoral journey through your beautiful land.

Mr. President. In responding to the kind words which you have addressed to me, I take the liberty of beginning with the passage from the prophet Micah that you quoted at your inauguration: "You have been told, Oh man, what is good, and what the Lord requires of you: only to do right and to love goodness, and to walk humbly with your God" (Mi. 6:8). In recalling these words, I wish to

greet you and all the authorities in the individual states
and in the nation who are committed to the good of the
citizens. There is indeed no other way to put oneself at
the service of the whole human person except by seeking
the good of every man and woman in all their commitments and activities.

Authority in the political community is based on the
objective ethical principle that the basic duty of power is
the solicitude of the common good of society and that it
serves the inviolable rights of the human person. The
individuals, families and various groups which compose
the civic community are aware that by themselves they
are unable to realize their human potential to the full,
and therefore they recognize in a wider community the
necessary condition for the ever better attainment of the
common good.

I wish to commend those in public authority and all the
people of the United States for having given, from the
very beginning of the existence of the nation, a special
place to some of the most important concerns of the
common good. Three years ago, during the bicentennial
celebration which I was fortunate to participate in as the
archbishop of Cracow, it was obvious to everyone that
concern for what is human and spiritual is one of the
basic principles governing the life of this community. It is
superfluous to add that respect for the freedom and the
dignity of every individual, whatever his origin, race, sex
or creed, has been a cherished tenet of the civil creed of
America, and that it has been backed up by courageous
decisions and actions.

Mr. President, ladies and gentlemen. I know and

appreciate this country's efforts for arms limitation, especially of nuclear weapons. Everyone is aware of the terrible risk that the stockpiling of such weapons brings upon humanity.

Disarmament

Since it is one of the greatest nations on earth, the United States plays a particularly important part in the quest for greater security in the world and for closer international collaboration. With all my heart I hope that there will be no relaxing of its efforts both to reduce the risk of a fatal and disastrous worldwide conflagration and to secure a prudent and progressive reduction of the destructive capacity of military arsenals.

At the same time, by reason of its special position, may the United States succeed in influencing the other nations to join in a continuing commitment for disarmament. Without wholeheartedly accepting such a commitment how can any nation effectively serve humanity, whose deepest desire is true peace?

Attachment to human values and to ethical concerns, which have been a hallmark of the American people, must be situated, especially in the present context of the growing interdependence of peoples across the globe, within the framework of the view that the common good of society embraces not just the individual nation to which one belongs but the citizens of the whole world. I would encourage every action for the reinforcement of peace in the world, a peace based on liberty and justice, on charity and truth.

Economic Development

The present-day relationships between peoples and between nations demand the establishment of greater international cooperation also in the economic field. The more powerful a nation is, the greater becomes its international responsibility; the greater also must be its commitment to the betterment of the lot of those whose very humanity is constantly being threatened by want and need. It is my fervent hope that all the powerful nations in the world will deepen their awareness of the principle of human solidarity within the one great human family.

America, which in the past decades has demonstrated goodness and generosity in providing food for the hungry of the world, will, I am sure, be able to match this generosity with an equally convincing contribution to the establishing of a world order that will create the necessary economic and trade conditions for a more just relationship between all the nations of the world, in respect for their dignity and their own personality.

Since people are suffering under international inequality, there can be no question of giving up the pursuit of international solidarity, even if it involves a notable change in the attitudes and lifestyles of those blessed with a larger share of the world's goods.

Mr. President, ladies and gentlemen. In touching upon the common good, which embodies the aspiration of all human beings to the full development of their capacities and the proper protection of their rights, I have dealt with areas where the Church that I represent and the political community that is the state share a common concern: the safeguarding of the dignity of the human person and the search for justice and peace. In their own proper spheres, the political community and the Church are mutually independent and self-governing. Yet, by a different title, each serves the personal and social vocation of the same human beings.

For her part, the Catholic Church will continue her efforts to cooperate in promoting justice, peace and dignity through the commitment of her leaders and the members of her communities, and through her incessant proclamation that all human beings are created to the image and likeness of God and that they are brothers and sisters, children of one heavenly Father.

May Almighty God bless and sustain America in her quest for the fullness of liberty, justice and peace.

The Rights and
Dignity of Man

*Speech before the Organization of American States,
Washington, October 6.*

Mr. President, Mr. Secretary General,
ladies and gentlemen.

1. It is indeed a pleasure for me to have this opportunity to greet all the distinguished representatives of the
different member nations of the Organization of
American States. My sincere gratitude goes to you,
Mr. President, for the cordial words of welcome you
have extended to me.

I thank also the secretary general for his thoughtful
invitation to come and visit the headquarters of the oldest
of the regional international organizations. It is fitting
that after my visit to the United Nations organization, the
Organization of American States should be the first one
among the many intergovernmental organizations and
agencies to which I am privileged to address a message of
peace and friendship.

The Holy See follows with great interest, and may I
say, with special attention, the events and developments

that touch upon the well-being of the peoples of the Americas. It felt, therefore, greatly honored by the invitation to send its own permanent observer to this institution—an invitation extended last year by a un-animous decision of the General Assembly.

The Holy See sees in regional organizations such as yours intermediary structures that promote a greater internal diversity and vitality in a given area within the global community of nations. The fact that the American continent is provided with an organization concerned with ensuring more continuity for the dialogue between governments, with promoting peace, with advancing full development in solidarity and with protecting man, his dignity and his rights, is a factor contributing to the health of the whole human family.

The Gospel and Christianity have entered deeply into your history and your cultures. I would like to call on this common tradition in order to present to you some reflections, in full respect for your personal convictions and your own competence, in order to bring to your endeavors an original contribution in a spirit of service.

The blessing of peace

2. Peace is a most precious blessing that you seek to preserve for your peoples. You are in agreement with me that it is not by accumulating arms that this peace can be ensured in a stable way. Apart from the fact that such accumulation increases in practice the danger of having recourse to arms to settle the disputes that may arise, it takes away considerable material and human resources

from the great peaceful tasks of development that are so urgent. It can also tempt some to think that the order built on arms is sufficient to ensure internal peace in the single countries.

I solemnly call on you to do everything in your power to restrain the arms race on this continent. There are no differences between your countries that cannot be peacefully overcome. What a relief it would be to your peoples, what new opportunities it would provide for their economic, social and cultural progress, and how contagious an example it would give the world, if the difficult enterprise of disarmament were here to find a realistic solution!

3. The painful experience of the history of my own country, Poland, has shown me how important national sovereignty is when it is served by a state worthy of the name and free in its decisions. How important it is for the protection not only of a people's legitimate material interests, but also of its culture and its soul. Your organization is an organization of states, founded on respect for the full national sovereignty of each, on equal participation in common tasks and on solidarity between your peoples.

Political rights

The legitimate demand by the states to participate on a basis of equality in the organization's common decisions must be matched by the will to promote within each country an ever more effective participation by the citizens in the responsibility and decisions of the nation, through ways that take into account particular traditions, difficulties and historical experiences.

4. However, while such difficulties and experiences can at times call for exceptional measures and a certain period of maturation in preparation for new advances in shared responsibility, they never, never justify any attack on the inviolable dignity of the human person and on the authentic rights that protect this dignity. If certain ideologies and certain ways of interpreting legitimate concern for national security were to result in subjugating to the state man and his rights and dignity, they would to that extent cease to be human and would be unable to claim without gross deception any Christian reference.

In the Church's thinking it is a fundamental principle that social organization is at the service of man, not vice versa. That holds good also for the highest levels of society where the power of coercion is wielded and where abuses, when they occur, are particularly serious. Besides, a security in which the people no longer feel involved, because it no longer protects them in their very humanity, is only a sham. As it grows more and more rigid, it will show symptoms of increasing weakness and rapidly approaching ruin.

Without undue interference, your organization can, by the spirit with which it tackles all the problems in its competence, do much throughout the continent to advance a concept of the state and its sovereignty that is truly human, and that is therefore the basis for the legitimacy of the states and of their acknowledged prerogatives for the service of man.

Man is the criterion

5. Man! Man is the decisive criterion that dictates and directs all your undertakings, the living value for whose service new initiatives are unceasingly demanded. The words that are most filled with meaning for man—words such as justice, peace, development, solidarity, human rights—are sometimes belittled as a result of systematic suspicion, or party and sectarian ideological censure. They then lose their power to mobilize and attract. They will recover it only if respect for the human person and commitment to the human person are explicitly brought back to the center of all considerations.

When we speak of the right to life, to physical and moral integrity, to nourishment, to housing, to education, to health care, to employment, to shared responsibility in the life of the nation, we speak of the human person. It is this human person whom faith makes us recognize as created in the image of God and destined for an eternal goal. It is this human person that is often threatened and hungry, without decent housing and employment, without access to the cultural heritage of his or her people or of humanity, and without a voice to make his or her distress heard.

The challenge of development

The great cause of full development in solidarity must be given new life by those who in one degree or another enjoy these blessings, for the service of all those—and there are many of them still on your continent—who are deprived of them to a sometimes dramatic extent.

6. The challenge of development deserves your full attention. In this field too what you achieve can be an example for humanity. The problems of rural and urban areas, of industry and agriculture, and of the environment are to a large extent a common task. The energetic pursuit of these will help to spread throughout the continent a sentiment of universal fraternity that extends beyond borders and regimes.

Without any disregard for the responsibilities of sovereign states, you discover that it is a logical requirement for you to deal with problems, such as unemployment, migration and trade, as common concerns whose continental dimension increasingly demands more organic solutions on a continental scale.

All that you do for the human person will halt violence and the threats of subversion and destabilization. For by accepting courageous revisions demanded by "this single fundamental point of view, namely the welfare of man— or, let us say, of the person in the community—which must, as a fundamental factor in the common good, constitute the essential criterion for all programs, systems and regimes" (*Redemptor Hominis,* 17), you direct the energies of your peoples toward the peaceful satisfaction of their aspirations.

7. The Holy See will always be happy to make its own disinterested contribution to this work. The local churches in the Americas will do the same within the framework of their various responsibilities. By advancing

the human person and his or her dignity and rights, they serve the earthly city, its cohesion and its lawful authorities. The full religious freedom that they ask for is in order to serve, not in order to oppose the legitimate autonomy of civil society and of its own means of action.

The more all citizens are able to exercise habitually their freedoms in the life of the nation, the more readily will the Christian communities be able to dedicate themselves to the central task of evangelization, namely the preaching of the Gospel of Jesus Christ, the source of life, strength, justice and peace.

(*Speaking in English*) With fervent prayers for prosperity and concord, I invoke upon this important assembly, upon the representatives of all the member states and their families, upon all the beloved peoples of the Americas, the choicest favors and blessings of Almighty God.

My visit here, in the Hall of the Americas, before this noble assembly dedicated to inter-American collaboration, expresses at the same time a wish and a prayer. My wish is that in all the nations of this continent, no man, woman or child may ever feel abandoned by the constituted authorities, to whom they are ready to accord their full confidence to the extent that those authorities seek the good of all. My prayer is that Almighty God may grant his light to the peoples and the governments, that they may always discover new means of collaboration for building up a fraternal and just society.

(*Speaking in Portuguese*) One last word before I leave you—with great regret—after this first brief visit to your esteemed organization.

When I visited Mexico, at the beginning of the year, I was amazed at the enthusiasm, spontaneity and joy of living of its people. I am convinced that you will succeed in preserving the rich human and cultural heritage of all your peoples and thus maintain the indispensable basis for true progress which is constituted, always and everywhere, by respect for the supreme dignity of man.

Fidelity to the Truth

Speech to the diplomatic corps in Washington, October 6.

Your excellencies, ladies and gentlemen: It pleases me greatly that in the midst of a program that is at the same time demanding and enjoyable, the opportunity has been offered to me to meet tonight with the distinguished members of the diplomatic corps in this city of Washington.

I thank you most cordially for the honor you bestow upon me by your presence, an honor given not only to my person but to the leader of the Catholic Church. I also see in your courteous gesture an encouragement for the activity of the Catholic Church and of the Holy See in the service of humanity.

In this cause of service to humanity the diplomatic corps and the Holy See stand together, each one in its own sphere, each one faithfully pursuing its own mission, but united in the great cause of understanding and solidarity among peoples and nations.

Yours is a noble task. Despite unavoidable difficulties, setbacks and failures, diplomacy retains its importance as one of the roads that must be traveled in the search for peace and progress for all mankind. "Diplomacy," in the words of my predecessor Paul VI, "is the art of making peace" (Address to the Diplomatic Corps, Rome, January 12, 1974).

The efforts of diplomats, whether in a bilateral or in a multilateral setting, do not always succeed in establishing or in maintaining peace, but they must always be encouraged, today as in the past, so that new initiatives will be born, new paths tried with the patience and tenacity that are the eminent qualities of the deserving diplomat.

As one who speaks in the name of Christ, who called himself "the way, the truth, and the life" (Jn. 14:6), I would also like to make a plea for the fostering of other qualities that are indispensable if today's diplomacy is to justify the hopes that are placed in it: the ever deeper insertion of the supreme values of the moral and spiritual order into the aims of peoples and into the methods used in pursuit of these aims.

The first imperative

First among the ethical imperatives that must preside over the relations among nations and peoples is truth. As the theme for the 13th World Day of Peace (January 1, 1980), I have chosen: "Truth, the Power of Peace." I am confident that the governments and the nations which you represent will, as they have so admirably done in the past, associate themselves once again with this lofty aim: to instill truth into all relationships, be they political or economic, bilateral or multinational.

All too often, falsehood is met in personal as well as in collective life, and thus suspicion arises where truth is called for, and the ensuing reluctance to enter into dialogue makes any collaboration or understanding almost impossible. Bringing truth into all relations is to work for peace, for it will make it possible to apply to the problems of the world the solutions that are in conformity with reason and with justice—in a word, with the truth about man.

And this brings me to the second point I would like to make. If it is to be true and lasting, peace must be truly human. The desire for peace is universal. It is embedded in the hearts of all human beings and it cannot be achieved unless the human person is placed at the center of every effort to bring about unity and brotherhood among nations.

Your mission as diplomats is based on the mandate you receive from those who hold responsibility for the well-being of your nations. The power you partake of cannot be separated from the objective demands of the moral order or from the destiny of every human being. May I repeat here what I stated in my first encyclical letter:

Objective and inviolable rights

"The fundamental duty of power is solicitude for the common good of society; this is what gives power its fundamental rights. Precisely in the name of these premises of the objective ethical order, the rights of power can only be understood on the basis of respect for the objective and inviolable rights of man. The common good that authority in the state serves is brought to full realization only when all the citizens are sure of their rights. The lack of this leads to the dissolution of society, opposition by citizens to authority or a situation of oppression, intimidation, violence and terrorism, of which many examples have been provided by the totalitarianisms of this century. Thus the principle of human rights is of profound concern to the area of social justice and is the measure by which it can be tested in the life of the political bodies'' (*Redemptor Hominis,* 17).

These considerations assume their full relevance also in the area of your immediate concern, the quest for international peace, for justice among nations and for cooperation in solidarity by all peoples. The success of today's diplomacy will, in the final analysis, be the victory of the truth about man.

I invoke from Almighty God abundant blessings upon your mission, which requires you to foster the interests of your own nation and to place it in the context of universal peace; upon you personally—who are in such a distinguished way artisans of peace; upon your spouses and families, who support and encourage you; and finally upon all who count on your dedicated service to see their own human dignity respected and enhanced. May God's peace be always in your hearts.

*An infant reaches out and touches the smiling face of John Paul II
as he leaves the National Shrine of the Immaculate Conception
in Washington, D.C., during the last day of his pilgrimage.*

Public Witness
and Inner Conversion

Address to women religious in Washington, October 7.

My first desire in this National Shrine of the Immaculate Conception is to direct my thoughts, to turn my heart to the woman of salvation history.

In the eternal design of God, this woman, Mary, was chosen to enter into the work of the incarnation and redemption. And this design of God was to be actuated through her free decision given in obedience to the divine will.

Through her yes—a yes that pervades and is reflected in all history, she consented to be the virgin mother of our saving God, the handmaid of the Lord and at the same time, the mother of all the faithful who in the course of centuries would become the brothers and sisters of her Son.

Through her, the Sun of Justice was to rise in the world. Through her, the great healer of humanity, the reconciler of hearts and consciences—her Son, the God-man Jesus Christ—was to transform the human condition and, by his death and resurrection, uplift the entire human family.

As a great sign that appeared in the heavens in the fullness of time, the woman dominates all history as the virgin mother of the Son, and as the spouse of the Holy Spirit—as the handmaid of humanity.

And the woman becomes also—by association with her Son—the sign of contradiction to the world and, at the same time, the sign of hope whom all generations shall call blessed: the woman who conceived spiritually before she conceived physically; the woman who accepted the word of God; the woman who was inserted intimately and irrevocably into the mystery of the Church, exercising a spiritual motherhood with regard to all people; the woman who is honored as Queen of Apostles, without herself being inserted into the hierarchical constitution of the Church. And yet this woman made all hierarchy possible, because she gave to the world the Shepherd and Bishop of our souls.

This woman, this Mary of the Gospels, who is not mentioned as being at the Last Supper, comes back again at the foot of the cross, in order to consummate her contribution to salvation history. By her courageous act, she prefigures and anticipates the courage of all women throughout the ages who concur in bringing forth Christ in every generation.

At Pentecost, the virgin mother once again comes forward to exercise her role in union with the apostles, with and in and over the Church. Yet again she conceives of the Holy Spirit, to bring forth Jesus in the fullness of his Body, the Church—never to leave him, never to abandon him, but to continue to love and serve him through the ages.

This is the woman of history and destiny, who inspires us today: the woman who speaks to us of femininity, human dignity and love, and who is the greatest expression of total consecration to Jesus Christ, in whose name we are gathered today.

Dear Sisters,

May the grace, love and peace of God our Father and our Lord Jesus Christ be with you.

I welcome this opportunity to speak with you today. I am happy for this occasion because of my esteem for religious life, and my gratitude to women religious for their invaluable contribution to the mission and very life of the Church.

I am especially pleased that we are gathered here in the National Shrine of the Immaculate Conception, for the Virgin Mary is the model of the Church, the mother of the faithful and the perfect example of consecrated life.

The greatest gift

1. On the day of our baptism, we received the greatest gift God can bestow on any man or woman. No other honor, no other distinction will equal its value. For we were freed from sin and incorporated into Christ Jesus and his body, the Church. That day and every day after, we were chosen "to live through love in his presence" (Eph. 1:4).

In the years that followed our baptism, we grew in awareness—even wonder—of the mystery of Christ. By listening to the Beatitudes, by meditating on the cross, conversing with Christ in prayer and receiving him in the Eucharist, we progressed toward the day, that particular moment of our life, when we solemnly ratified with full awareness and freedom our baptismal consecration. We affirmed our determination to live always in union with Christ, and to be, according to the gifts given us by the Holy Spirit, a generous and loving member of the people of God.

2. Your religious consecration builds on this common foundation which all Christians share in the Body of Christ. Desiring to perfect and intensify what God had begun in your life by baptism, and discerning that God was indeed offering you the gift of the evangelical counsels, you willed to follow Christ more closely, to conform your life more completely to that of Jesus Christ, in and through a distinctive religious community.

This is the essence of religious consecration: to profess within and for the benefit of the Church, poverty, chastity and obedience in response to God's special invitation, in order to praise and serve God in greater freedom of heart (cf. 1 Cor. 7:34-35) and to have one's life more closely conformed to Christ in the manner of life chosen by him and his blessed mother. (cf. *Perfectae Caritatis,* 1; *Lumen Gentium,* 46).

A distinctive way

3. Religious consecration not only deepens your personal commitment to Christ, but it also strengthens your relationship to his spouse, the Church. Religious consecration is a distinctive manner of living in the Church, a particular way of fulfilling the life of faith and service begun in baptism.

On her part, the Church assists you in your discernment of God's will. Having accepted and authenticated the charisms of your various institutes, she then unites your religious profession to the celebration of Christ's paschal mystery.

You are called by Jesus himself to verify and manifest in your lives and in your activities your deepened relationship with his Church. This bond of union with the Church must also be shown in the spirit and apostolic endeavors of every religious institute. For faithfulness to Christ, especially in religious life, can never be separated from faithfulness to the Church.

This ecclesial dimension of the vocation of religious consecration has many important practical consequences for institutes themselves and for each individual member. It implies, for example, a greater public witness to the Gospel, since you represent, in a special way as women religious, the spousal relationship of the Church to Christ.

Fidelity to founders' charisms

The ecclesial dimension also requires, on the part of individual members as well as entire institutes, a faithfulness to the original charisms which God has given to his Church, through your founders and foundresses.

It means that institutes are called to continue to foster, in dynamic faithfulness, those corporate commitments which were related to the original charism, which were authenticated by the Church, and which still fulfill important needs of the people of God. A good example in this regard would be the Catholic school system which has been invaluable for the Church in the United States, an excellent means not only for communicating the Gospel of Christ to the students, but also for permeating the entire community with Christ's truth and his love. It is one of the apostolates in which women religious have made, and are still making an incomparable contribution.

4. Dear sisters in Christ: Jesus must always be first in your lives. His person must be at the center of your activities—the activities of every day.

No other person and no other activity can take precedence over him. For your whole life has been consecrated to him. With St. Paul you have to say: "All I want is to know Christ and the power of his resurrection and to share his sufferings by reproducing the pattern of his death" (Phil. 3:10).

Christ remains primary in your life only when he enjoys the first place in your mind and heart. Thus you must continuously unite yourself to him in prayer.

Need for prayer

Without prayer, religious life has no meaning. It has lost contact with its source, it has emptied itself of substance and it no longer can fulfill its goal. Without prayer there can be no joy, no hope, no peace. For prayer is what keeps us in touch with Christ. The incisive words written in *Evangelica Testificatio* cause us all to reflect, "Do not forget the witness of history: faithfulness to prayer or its abandonment is the test of the vitality or decadence of religious life" (*Evangelica Testificatio,* 42).

5. Two dynamic forces are operative in religious life: your love for Jesus—and, in Jesus, for all who belong to him—and his love for you.

We cannot live without love. If we do not encounter love, if we do not experience it and make it our own, and if we do not participate intimately in it, our life is meaningless. Without love we remain incomprehensible to ourselves (cf. *Redemptor Hominis*, 10).

Thus every one of you needs a vibrant relationship of love to the Lord, a profound loving union with Christ, your Spouse, a love like that expressed in the Psalm: "God, you are my God whom I seek, for you my flesh pines and my soul thirsts like the earth, parched, lifeless and without water. Thus have I gazed toward you in the sanctuary to see your power and your glory" (Ps. 63:1-2).

Yet far more important than your love for Christ is God's love for you. You have been called by him, made a member of his Body, consecrated in a life of the evangelical counsels and destined by him to have a share in the mission that Christ has entrusted to the Church: his mission of salvation.

A Eucharistic life

For this reason, you center your life on the Eucharist. In the Eucharist, you celebrate his death and resurrection and receive from him the Bread of eternal life. And it is in the Eucharist especially that you are united to the one who is the object of all your love. Here, with him, you find ever greater reasons to love and serve his brothers and sisters. Here, with him—with Christ—you find greater understanding and compassion for God's people. And here you find the strength to persevere in your commitment to selfless service.

6. Your service in the Church is then an extension of Christ to whom you have dedicated your life. For it is not yourself that you put forward, but Christ Jesus as Lord. Like John the Baptist, you know that for Christ to increase, you must decrease. And so your life must be characterized by a complete availability: a readiness to serve as the needs of the Church require, a readiness to give public witness to the Christ whom you love.

The need for this public witness becomes a constant call to inner conversion, to justice and holiness of life on the part of each religious. It also becomes an invitation to each institute to reflect on the purity of its corporate ecclesial witness. And it is for this reason that in my address last November to the International Union of Superiors General, I mentioned that it is not unimportant that your consecration to God should be manifested in the permanent exterior sign of a simple and suitable religious garb. This is not only my personal conviction, but also the desire of the Church, often expressed by so many of the faithful.

Adherence to the magisterium

As daughters of the Church—a title cherished by so many of your great saints—you are called to a generous and loving adherence to the authentic magisterium of the Church, which is a solid guarantee of the fruitfulness of all your apostolates and an indispensable condition for the proper interpretation of the "signs of the times."

7. The contemplative life occupies today and forever a place of great honor in the Church. The prayer of contemplation was found in the life of Jesus himself, and has been a part of religious life in every age. I take this opportunity therefore—as I did in Rome, in Mexico and in Poland—to encourage again all who are members of contemplative communities.

Know that you shall always fulfill an important place in the church, in her mission of salvation, in her service to the whole community of the people of God. Continue faithfully, confidently and prayerfully, in the rich tradition that has been handed down to you.

In closing, I remind you, with sentiments of admiration and love, that the aim of religious life is to render praise and glory to the most Holy Trinity, and, through your consecration, to help humanity enter into fullness of life in the Father, and in the Son and in the Holy Spirit.

In all your planning and in all your activities, try also to keep this aim before you. There is no greater service you can give; there is no greater fulfillment you can receive.

Dear sisters: today and forever: Praised be Jesus Christ.

Prayer to Mary

This shrine speaks to us with the voice of all America, with the voice of all the sons and daughters of America, who have come here from the various countries of the Old World. When they came, they brought with them in their hearts the same love for the Mother of God that was a characteristic of their ancestors and of themselves in their native lands.

These people, speaking different languages, coming from different backgrounds of history and tradition in their own countries, came together around the heart of a Mother whom they all had in common. While their faith in Christ made all of them aware of being the one people of God, this awareness became all the more vivid through the presence of the Mother in the work of Christ and the Church.

Today, as I thank you, Mother, for this presence of yours in the midst of the men and women of this land—a presence which has lasted 200 years—giving a new form to their social and civic lives in the United States, I commend them all to your immaculate heart.

With gratitude and joy I recall that you have been honored as patroness of the United States, under the title of your Immaculate Conception since the days of the Sixth Provincial Council of Baltimore in 1846.

I commend to you, Mother of Christ, and I entrust to you, the Catholic Church: the bishops, priests, deacons, individual religious and religious institutes, the seminarians, vocations and the apostolate of the laity in its various aspects.

In a special way, I entrust to you the well-being of the Christian families of this country, the innocence of children, the future of the young, the vocation of single men and women. I ask you to communicate to all the women of the United States a deep sharing in the joy that you experienced in your closeness to Jesus Christ, your

Son. I ask you to preserve all of them in freedom from sin and evil, like the freedom which was yours in a unique way from that moment of supreme liberation in your Immaculate Conception.

I entrust to you the great work of ecumenism here, in this land, in which those who confess Christ belong to different churches and communions. I do this in order that the words of Christ's prayer may be fulfilled: "That they may be one."

I entrust to you the consciences of men and women and the voice of public opinion, in order that they may not be opposed to the law of God but follow it as the fount of truth and good.

I add to this, Mother, the great cause of justice and peace in the modern world, in order that the force and energy of love may prevail over hatred and destructiveness, and in order that the children of light may not lack concern for the welfare of the whole family.

Mother, I commend and entrust to you all that goes to make up earthly progress, asking that it should not be one-sided but that it should create conditions for the full spiritual advancement of individuals, families, communities and nations.

I commend to you the poor, the suffering, the sick and the handicapped, the aging and the dying.

I ask you to reconcile those in sin, to heal those in pain, and to uplift those who have lost their hope and joy. Show to those who struggle in doubt the light of Christ your Son.

Bishops of the Church in the United States have chosen your Immaculate Conception as the mystery to hold the patronage over the people of God in this land. May the hope contained in this mystery overcome sin and be shared by all the sons and daughters of America, and also by the whole human family.

At a time when the struggle between good and evil, between the prince of darkness and father of lies and evangelical love is growing more acute, may the light of your Immaculate Conception show to all the way to grace and to salvation. Amen.

Academic Excellence
and Christian Truth

Address to Catholic educators in Washington, October 6.

Dear brothers and sisters in Christ.

1. Our meeting today gives me great pleasure, and I thank you sincerely for your cordial welcome. My own association with the university world, and more particularly with the Pontifical Theological Faculty of Cracow, makes our encounter all the more gratifying for me. I cannot but feel at home with you.

The sincere expressions with which the chancellor and the president of the Catholic University of America have confirmed, in the name of all of you, the faithful adherence to Christ and the generous commitment to the service of truth and charity of your Catholic associations and institutions of higher learning are appreciated.

Ninety-one years ago Cardinal Gibbons and the American bishops requested the foundation of the Catholic University of America, as a university "destined to provide the Church with worthy ministers for the salvation of souls and the propagation of religions and to give the republic most worthy citizens." It seems appropriate to me on this occasion to address myself not only to this great institution, so irrevocably linked to the bishops of the United States, who have founded it and who generously support it, but also to all the Catholic universities, colleges and academies of post-secondary learning in your land, those with formal and sometimes juridical links with the Holy See, as well as all those who are "Catholic."

2. Before doing so, though, allow me first to mention the ecclesiastical faculties, three of which are established here at the Catholic University of America. I greet these faculties and all who dedicate their best talents in them.

I offer my prayers for the prosperous development and the unfailing fidelity and success of these faculties. In the apostolic constitution *Sapientia Christiana,* I have dealt directly with these institutions in order to provide guidance and to ensure that they fulfill their role in meeting the needs of the Christian community in today's rapidly changing circumstances.

I also wish to address a word of praise and admiration for the men and women, especially priests and religious, who dedicate themselves to all forms of campus ministry. Their sacrifices and efforts to bring the true message of Christ to the university world, whether secular or Catholic, cannot go unnoticed.

The Church also greatly appreciates the work and witness of those of her sons and daughters whose vocation places them in non-Catholic universities in your country. I am sure that their Christian hope and Catholic patrimony bring an enriching and irreplaceable dimension to the world of higher studies.

A special word of gratitude and appreciation also goes to the parents and students who, sometimes at the price of great personal and financial sacrifice, look toward the Catholic universities and colleges for the training that unites faith and science, culture and the Gospel values.

To all engaged in administration, teaching or study in Catholic colleges and universities I would apply the words of Daniel: "They who are learned shall shine like the brightness of the firmament and those that instruct many in justice as stars for all eternity" (Dn. 12:3). Sacrifice and generosity have accomplished heroic results in the foundation and development of these institutions. Despite immense financial strain, enrollment problems and other obstacles, Divine Providence and the commitment of the whole people of God have allowed us to see these Catholic institutions flourish and advance.

Three aims to pursue

3. I would repeat here before you what I told the professors and students of the Catholic universities in Mexico when I indicated three aims that are to be pursued. A Catholic university or college must make a specific contribution to the Church and to society through high-quality scientific research, in-depth study of problems, and a just sense of history, together with the concern to show the full meaning of the human person regenerated in Christ, thus favoring the complete development of the person.

Furthermore, the Catholic university or college must train young men and women of outstanding knowledge who, having made a personal synthesis between faith and culture, will be both capable and willing to assume tasks in the service of the community and of society in general, and to bear witness to their faith before the world. And finally, to be what it ought to be, a Catholic college or university must set up, among its faculty and students, a real community which bears witness to a living and operative Christianity, a community where sincere commitment to scientific research and study goes together with a deep commitment to authentic Christian living.

This is your identity. This is your vocation. Every university or college is qualified by a specific mode of being. Yours is the qualification of being Catholic, of affirming God, his revelation and the Catholic Church as the guardian and interpreter of that revelation. The term "Catholic" will never be a mere label, either added or dropped according to the pressures of varying factors.

Surrender to objectivity

4. As one who for long years has been a university professor, I will never tire of insisting on the eminent role of the university, which is to instruct but also to be a place of scientific research. In both these fields, its activity is closely related to the deepest and noblest aspiration of the human person: the desire to come to the knowledge of truth.

No university can deserve the rightful esteem of the world of learning unless it applies the highest standards of scientific research, constantly updating its methods and working instruments, and unless it excels in seriousness and therefore in freedom of investigation. Truth and science are not gratuitous conquests, but the result of a surrender to objectivity and of the exploration of all aspects of nature and man.

Whenever man himself becomes the object of investigation, no single method or combination of methods can fail to take into account, beyond any purely natural approach, the full nature of man. Because he is bound by the total truth on man, the Christian will, in his research and in his teaching, reject any partial vision of human reality, but he will let himself be enlightened by his faith in the creation of God and the redemption of Christ.

The relationship to truth explains therefore the historical bond between the university and the Church. Because she herself finds her origin and her growth in the words of Christ, which are the liberating truth (cf. Jn. 8:32), the Church has always tried to stand by the institutions that serve, and cannot but serve, the knowledge of truth.

The Church can rightfully boast of being in a sense the mother of universities. The names of Bologna, Padua, Prague and Paris shine in the earliest history of intellectual endeavor and human progress. The continuity of the historic tradition in this field has come down to our day.

Evangelization and service

5. An undiminished dedication to intellectual honesty and academic excellence are seen, in a Catholic university, in the perspective of the Church's mission of evan-

gelization and service. This is why the Church asks these institutions, your institutions, to set out without equivocation your Catholic nature. This is what I have desired to emphasize in my apostolic constitution *Sapientia Christiana,* where I stated:

"Indeed, the Church's mission of spreading the Gospel not only demands that the good news be preached ever more widely and to ever greater numbers of men and women, but that the very power of the Gospel should permeate thought patterns, standards of judgment and the norms of behavior. In a word, it is necessary that the whole of human culture be steeped in the Gospel. The cultural atmosphere in which a human being lives has a great influence upon his or her way of thinking and, thus, of acting. Therefore, a division between faith and culture is more than a small impediment to evangelization, while a culture penetrated with the Christian spirit is an instrument that favors the spreading of the good news" (*Sapientia Christiana,* I).

The goals of Catholic higher education go beyond education for production, professional competence, technological and scientific competence. They aim at the ultimate destiny of the human person, at the full justice and holiness born of truth (cf. Eph. 4:24).

6. If then your universities and colleges are institutionally committed to the Christian message, and if they are part of the Catholic community of evangelization, it follows that they have an essential relationship to the hierarchy of the Church. And here I want to say a special word of gratitude, encouragement and guidance for the theologians.

The Church needs her theologians, particularly in this time and age so profoundly marked by deep changes in all areas of life and society. The bishops of the Church, to whom the Lord has entrusted the keeping of the unity of the faith and the preaching of the message—individual bishops for their dioceses, and bishops collegially with the successor of Peter for the universal Church—we all need your work, your dedication and the fruits of your reflection. We desire to listen to you and we are eager to receive the valued assistance of your responsible scholarship.

The rights of the faithful

But true theological scholarship, and by the same token theological teaching, cannot exist and be fruitful without seeking its inspiration and its source in the word of God as contained in Sacred Scripture and in the sacred tradition of the Church, as interpreted by the authentic magisterium throughout history (cf. *Dei Verbum,* 10). True academic freedom must be seen in relation to the finality of the academic enterprise which looks to the total truth of the human person.

The theologian's contribution will be enriching for the Church only if it takes into account the proper function of the bishops and the rights of the faithful. It devolves upon the bishops of the Church to safeguard the Christian authenticity and unity of faith and moral teaching, in accordance with the injunction of the Apostle Paul: "Proclaim the message and, welcome or unwelcome, insist on it. Refute falsehood, correct error, call to obedience..." (2 Tim. 4:2).

It is the right of the faithful not to be troubled by theories and hypotheses that they are not expert in judging or that are easily simplified or manipulated by public opinion for ends that are alien to the truth. On the day of his death, John Paul I stated: "Among the rights of the faithful, one of the greatest is the right to receive God's word in all its entirety and purity..." (Sept. 28, 1979).

It behooves the theologian to be free, but with the freedom that is openness to the truth and the light that comes from faith and from fidelity to the Church.

In concluding I express to you once more my joy in being with you today. I remain very close to your work and your concerns. May the Holy Spirit guide you. May the intercession of Mary, seat of wisdom, sustain you always in your irreplaceable service of humanity and the Church. God bless you.

A unity of Love
and Hope

Address to an ecumenical meeting at Trinity College, Washington, October 7.

Dearly beloved in Christ,

1. I am grateful to the providence of God that permits me, on my visit to the United States of America, to have this meeting with other religious leaders, and to be able to join with you in prayer for the unity of all Christians.

It is indeed fitting that our meeting should occur just a short time before the observance of the 15th anniversary of the Second Vatican Council's Decree on Ecumenism, *Unitatis Redintegratio.* Since the inception of my pontificate, almost a year ago, I have endeavored to devote myself to the service of Christian unity. For, as I stated in my first encyclical, it is certain "that in the present historical situation of Christianity and of the world, the only possibility we see in fulfilling the Church's universal mission, with regard to ecumenical questions, is that of seeking sincerely, perseveringly, humbly and also courageously the ways of drawing closer and of union" (*Redemptor Hominis,* 6).

On a previous occasion, I said that the problem of division within Christianity is "binding in a special way on the bishop of the ancient church of Rome, founded on the preaching and the testimonies of the martyrdom of Sts. Peter and Paul" (General Audience, Jan. 17, 1979). And today I wish to reiterate before you the same conviction.

2. With great satisfaction and joy I welcome the opportunity to embrace you, in the charity of Christ, as beloved Christian brethren and fellow disciples of the Lord Jesus. It is a privilege to be able, in your presence and together with you, to give expression to the testimony of John, that "Jesus Christ is the Son of God" (1 Jn. 4:15), and to proclaim that "there is one mediator between God and men, the man Christ Jesus" (1 Tim. 2:5).

In the united confession of faith in the divinity of Jesus Christ, we feel great love for each other and great hope for all humanity. We experience immense gratitude to the Father, who has sent his Son to be our Savior, "the expiation for our sins, and not for ours only but for the sins of the whole world" (1 Jn. 2:2).

Christ's prayer for unity

By divine grace we are united in esteem and love for Sacred Scripture, which we recognize as the inspired word of God. And it is precisely in this word of God that we learn how much he wants us to be fully one in him and in his Father. Jesus prays that his followers may be one "so that the world may believe...'" (Jn. 17:21). That the credibility of evangelization should, by God's plan, depend on the unity of his followers is a subject of inexhaustible meditation for all of us.

3. I wish to pay homage here to the many splendid ecumenical initiatives that have been realized in this country through the action of the Holy Spirit. In the last 15 years there has been a positive response to ecumenism by the bishops of the United States. Through their committee for ecumenical and interreligious affairs, they have established a fraternal relationship with other churches and ecclesial communities—a relationship which, I pray, will continue to deepen in the coming years. Conversations are in progress with our brothers from the East, the Orthodox. Here I wish to note that this relationship has been strong in the United States and that soon a theological dialogue will begin on a world-wide basis in an attempt to resolve those difficulties which hinder full unity.

There are also American dialogues with the Anglicans, the Lutherans, the Reformed churches, the Methodists and the Disciples of Christ—all having a counterpart on the international level. A fraternal exchange exists likewise between the Southern Baptists and American theologians.

My gratitude goes to all who collaborate in the matter of joint theological investigation, the aim of which is always the full evangelical and Christian dimension of truth. It is to be hoped that, through such investigation, persons who are well-prepared by a solid grounding in their own traditions will contribute to a deepening of the full historical and doctrinal understanding of the issues.

The particular climate and traditions of the United States have been conducive to joint witness in the defense of the rights of the human person, in the pursuit of goals of social justice and peace and in questions of public morality. These areas of concern must continue to benefit from creative ecumenical action, as must the fostering of esteem for the sacredness of marriage and the support of a healthy family life as a major contribution to the well-being of the nation. In this context, recognition must be given to the deep division which still exists over moral and ethical matters. The moral life and the life of faith are so deeply united that it is impossible to divide them.

4. Much has been accomplished but there is still much to be done. We must go forward, however, with a spirit of hope. Even the very desire for the complete unity in faith—which is lacking between us, and which must be achieved before we can lovingly celebrate the Eucharist together in truth—is itself a gift of the Holy Spirit, for which we offer humble praise to God. We are confident that through our common prayer the Lord Jesus will lead us, at the moment dependent on the sovereign action of his Holy Spirit, to the fullness of ecclesial unity.

Interior conversion and prayer

Faithfulness to the Holy Spirit calls for interior conversion and fervent prayer. In the words of the Second Vatican Council: "This change of heart and holiness of life, along with public and private prayer for the unity of Christians, should be regarded as the soul of the whole ecumenical movement..." (*Unitatis Redintegratio,* 8).

It is important that every individual Christian search

his or her heart to see what may obstruct the attainment of full union among Christians. And let us all pray that the genuine need for the patience to await God's hour will never occasion complacency in the status quo of division in faith. By divine grace may the need for patience never become a substitute for the definitive and generous response which God asks that there be given to his invitation to perfect unity in Christ.

And so, as we are gathered here to celebrate the love of God that is poured out in our hearts by the Holy Spirit let us be conscious of the call to show supreme fidelity to the will of Christ. Let us together perseveringly ask the Holy Spirit to remove all divisions from our faith, to give us that perfect unity in truth and love for which Christ prayed, for which Christ died: "to gather together in unity the scattered children of God" (Jn. 11:52).

I offer my respectful greeting of grace and peace to those whom you represent, to each of your respective congregations, to all who long for the coming of "our great God and savior Jesus Christ" (Ti. 2:14).

Forming and Informing
World Public Opinion

Remarks to journalists in Washington, October 7.

My dear friends of the communications media. Here we are together again at the end of another journey—a journey which this time has brought me to Ireland, to the United Nations and to the United States of America.

The purpose of this journey was to permit the Pope to exercise his function as a herald of peace, in the name of Christ, who was referred to as the Prince of Peace. This message of peace was announced especially in those places and before those audiences where the problem of war and peace is perceived with particular sensitivity and where there exist the conditions of understanding, of good will and of the means necessary to building peace and cooperation among all nations and among all peoples.

The word "peace" is a synthesis. It has many components. I have touched on several of these during this journey, and you have diligently reported on these reflections. You have commented on them; you have interpreted them; you have performed the service of stimulating people to think about how they might contribute to a firmer foundation for peace, for cooperation and for justice among all persons.

Now we find ourselves at the moment of parting, in this capital city of one of the most powerful nations in the world. The power of this country, I believe, comes not only from material wealth but from a richness of spirit.

In fact, the name of this city and of the tall monument which dominates it recalls the spirit of George Washington, the first president of the nation, who—with Thomas Jefferson, for whom an imposing memorial also exists here, and with other enlightened individuals—established this country on a foundation which was not only human but also profoundly religious.

As a consequence, the Catholic Church has been able to flourish here. The millions of faithful who belong to the Church testify to that fact as they exercise the rights and duties which flow from their faith with full freedom. The great National Shrine of the Immaculate Conception in this city testifies to that fact. The existence in this capital city of two Catholic universities—Georgetown and the Catholic University of America—testifies to that fact. I have observed that the people of the United States of America proudly and gratefully pledge allegiance to their republic as "one nation under God."

Cause to reflect

This one nation is made up of many members—members of all races, of all religions, of all conditions of life—so that it is a type of microcosm of the world community and accurately reflects the motto, *E Pluribus Unum*. As

203

this country courageously abolished the plague of slavery under the presidency of Abraham Lincoln, may it never stop striving for the effective good of all the inhabitants of this one nation and of that unity which reflects its national motto. For this reason, the United States of America gives to all cause to reflect on a spirit which, if well applied, can bring beneficial results for peace in the world community.

I sincerely hope that all of you have profited from this journey, and that you have had the opportunity to reflect anew on the values which have come from Christianity to the civilization of this new continent. Most of all, however, we can draw hope for a peaceful world community from the example of persons of all races, of all nationalities and of all religions living together in peace and unity.

As we prepare to part, my dear friends, I am consoled by the fact that you will continue to inform and to form world public opinion with a profound consciousness of your responsibility and with the realization that so many persons depend on you.

Finally, I say goodbye to you and to America. I thank you again, and with all my heart I ask God to bless you and your families.

The Specific
Role of the Laity

*Address to leaders of the Knights of Columbus
in Washington, October 7.*

It gives me great pleasure to be with you on the occasion of my pastoral visit to the United States. I thank you most sincerely for the respect and love which you have manifested toward me as successor of Peter, bishop of Rome and pastor of the universal Church.

In the person of the supreme knight and the members of the supreme board, I greet all the Knights of Columbus, the more than 1,300,000 Catholic laymen all over the world, who display a spirit of profound attachment to their Christian faith and of loyalty to the Apostolic See.

Many times in the past, and again today, you have given expression to your solidarity with the mission of the Pope. I see in your support a further proof—if further proof were ever necessary—of your awareness that the Knights of Columbus highly value their vocation to be part of the evangelization effort of the Church. I am happy to recall here what my revered predecessor, Paul VI, said about this task in his apostolic exhortation,

"Evangelii Nuntiandi," as he emphasized the specific role of the laity: "Their own field of evangelization activity is the vast and complicated world of politics, society and economics, but also the world of culture, of the sciences and the arts, of international life, of the mass media. It also includes other realities which are open to evangelization, such as human love, the family, the education of children and adolescents, professional work and suffering." (no. 70)

These words of one who never ceased to encourage you clearly indicate the road which your association must travel. I am aware of the many efforts you make to promote the use of mass media for the spreading of the Gospel and for the wider diffusion of my own messages. May the Lord reward you, and through your efforts bring forth abundant fruits of evangelization in the Church. May your dedicated activity in turn help you realize in yourselves those interior attitudes without which no one can truly evangelize: trust in the power of the Holy Spirit, true holiness of life, deep concern for truth, and an ever increasing love for all God's children.

Striding briskly across the platform in front of the altar on the Washington, D.C., Mall, the Pope extends his arms in farewell to the throngs.

P. Gnemmi

"Stand Up" for Human Life

Homily of the Mass on the Mall, Washington, October 7.

Dear brothers and sisters in Jesus Christ,

1. In his dialogue with his listeners, Jesus was faced one day with an attempt by some Pharisees to get him to endorse their current views regarding the nature of marriage.

Jesus answered by reaffirming the teaching of scripture: "At the beginning of creation God made them male and female; for this reason a man shall leave his father and mother and the two shall become one. They are no longer two but one in flesh. Therefore let no man separate what God has joined" (Mk. 10:6-9).

The Gospel according to Mark immediately adds the description of a scene with which we are all familiar. This scene shows Jesus becoming indignant when he noticed how his own disciples tried to prevent the people from bringing their children closer to him. And so he said: "Let the children come to me and do not hinder them. It is to just such as these that the kingdom of God belongs... Then he embraced them and blessed them, placing his hands on them'' (Mk. 10:14-16).

In proposing these readings, today's liturgy invites all of us to reflect on the nature of marriage, on the family and on the value of life—three themes that are so closely interconnected.

2. I shall all the more gladly lead you in reflecting on the word of God as proposed by the Church today, because all over the world the bishops are discussing marriage and family life as they are lived in all dioceses and nations. The bishops are doing this in preparation for the next World Synod of Bishops, which has as its theme: ''The Role of the Christian Family in the Contemporary World.''

Your own bishops have designated next year as a year of study, planning and pastoral renewal with regard to the family. For a variety of reasons there is a renewed interest throughout the world in marriage, in family life and in the value of all human life.

All human life is sacred

This very Sunday marks the beginning of the annual Respect Life program, through which the Church in the United States intends to reiterate its conviction regarding the inviolability of human life in all stages. Let us then, all together, renew our esteem for the value of human life, remembering also that, through Christ, all human life has been redeemed.

3. I do not hesitate to proclaim before you and before the world that all human life—from the moment of concep-

tion and through all subsequent stages—is sacred, because human life is created in the image and likeness of God.

Nothing surpasses the greatness of dignity of a human person. Human life is not just an idea or an abstraction. Human life is the concrete reality of a being that lives, that acts, that grows and develops. Human life is the concrete reality of a being that is capable of love and of service to humanity.

Let me repeat what I told the people during my recent pilgrimage to my homeland: "If a person's right to life is violated at the moment in which he is first conceived in his mother's womb, an indirect blow is struck also at the whole of the moral order which serves to ensure the inviolable goods of man. Among those goods, life occupies the first place.

The Church defends the right to life, not only in regard to the majesty of the Creator, who is the first giver of this life, but also in respect of the essential good of the human person" (June 8, 1979).

4. Human life is precious because it is the gift of a God whose love is infinite; and when God gives life, it is forever. Life is also precious because it is the expression and the fruit of love. This is why life should spring up within the setting of marriage, and why marriage and the partners' love for one another should be marked by generosity in self-giving.

The great danger for family life in the midst of any society whose idols are pleasure, comfort and independence, lies in the fact that people close their hearts and become selfish. The fear of making permanent commitments can change the mutual love of husband and wife into two of self—two loves existing side by side, until they end in separation.

In the sacrament of marriage, a man and a woman—who at baptism became members of Christ and hence have the duty of manifesting Christ's attitudes in their lives—are assured of the help they need to develop their love in a faithful and indissoluble union and to respond with generosity to the gift of parenthood. As the Second Vatican Council declared: Through this sacrament, Christ himself becomes present in the life of the married couple and accompanies them, so that they may love each other and their children, just as Christ loved his Church by giving himself up for her (cf. *Gaudium et Spes, 48;* cf. Eph. 5:25).

A demanding vocation

5. In order that Christian marriage may favor the total good and development of the married couple, it must be inspired by the Gospel, and thus be open to new life—new life to be given and accepted generously. The couple is also called to create a family atmosphere in which children can be happy and lead full and worthy human and Christian lives.

To maintain a joyful family requires much from both the parents and the children. Each member of the family has to become, in a special way, the servant of the others and share their burdens (cf. Gal. 6:2; Phil. 2:2). Each one must show concern, not only for his or her own life, but also for the lives of the other members of the family: their needs, their hopes, their ideals.

Decisions about the number of children and the sacrifices to be made for them must not be taken only with a view to adding to comfort and preserving a peaceful existence. Reflecting upon this matter before God, with the graces drawn from the sacrament and guided by the teaching of the Church, parents will remind themselves that it is certainly less serious to deny their children certain comforts or material advantages than to deprive them of the presence of brothers and sisters who could help them to grow in humanity and to realize the beauty of life at all its ages and in all its variety.

If parents fully realized the demands and the opportunities that this great sacrament brings, they could not fail to join in Mary's hymn to the Author of Life—to God—who has made them his chosen fellow workers.

All human beings ought to value every person for his or her uniqueness as a creature of God, called to be a brother or sister of Christ by reason of the incarnation and the universal redemption. For us, the sacredness of human life is based on these premises. And it is on these same premises that there is based our celebration of life— all human life. This explains our efforts to defend human life against every influence or action that threatens or weakens it, as well as our endeavors to make every life more human in all its aspects.

When life is threatened

And so, we will stand up every time that human life is threatened.

• When the sacredness of life before birth is attacked,

we will stand up and proclaim that no one ever has the authority to destroy unborn life.

• When a child is described as a burden or looked upon only as a means to satisfy an emotional need, we will stand up and insist that every child is a unique and unrepeatable gift of God, with the right to a loving and united family.

• When the institution of marriage is abandoned to human selfishness or reduced to a temporary, conditional arrangement that can easily be terminated, we will stand up and affirm the indissolubility of the marriage bond.

• When the value of the family is threatened because of social and economic pressures, we will stand up and reaffirm that the family is "necessary not only for the private good of every person, but also for the common good of every society, nation and state" (General Audience, January 3, 1979).

• When freedom is used to dominate the weak, to squander natural resources and energy, and to deny basic necessities to people, we will stand up and reaffirm the demands of justice and social love.

• When the sick, the aged or the dying are abandoned in loneliness, we will stand up and proclaim that they are worthy of love, care and respect.

I make my own the words which Paul VI spoke last year to the American bishops:

"We are convinced, moreover, that all efforts made to safeguard human rights actually benefit life itself. Everything aimed at banishing discrimination—in law or in fact—which is based on race, origin, color, culture, sex or religion (cf. *Octogesima Adveniens,* 16) is a service to life. When the rights of minorities are fostered, when the mentally or physically handicapped are assisted, when those on the margin of society are given a voice—in all these instances the dignity of life and the sacredness of human life are furthered... In particular, every contribution made to better the moral climate of society, to oppose permissiveness and hedonism, and all assistance to the family, which is the source of new life, effectively uphold the values of life" (May 26, 1978).

Courage is needed

Much remains to be done to support those whose lives are wounded and to restore hope to those who are afraid of life. Courage is needed to resist pressures and false slogans, to proclaim the supreme dignity of all life, and to demand that society itself give it its protection.

A distinguished American, Thomas Jefferson, once stated: "The care of human life and happiness and not their destruction is the just and only legitimate object of good government" (March 31, 1809). I wish therefore to praise all the members of the Catholic Church and other Christian churches, all men and women of the Judaeo-Christian heritage, as well as all people of good will who unite in common dedication for the defense of life in its fullness and for the promotion of all human rights.

Our celebration of life forms part of the celebration of the Eucharist. Our Lord and Savior, through his death and resurrection, has become for us "the Bread of Life" and the pledge of eternal life. In him we find the courage, perseverance and inventiveness which we need to promote and defend life within our families and throughout the world.

Dear brothers and sisters: We are confident that Mary, the Mother of God and the Mother of Life, will give us her help so that our way of living will always, reflect our admiration and gratitude for God's gift of love that is life. We know that she will help us to use every day that is given to us as an opportunity to defend the life of the unborn and to render more human the lives of all our fellow human beings, wherever they may be.

And through the intercession of Our Lady of the Rosary, whose feast we celebrate today, may we come one day to the fullness of eternal life in Christ Jesus our Lord. Amen.